British sitcoms have a unique charm that has captivated audiences for decades. From the bumbling antics of "Only Fools and Horses" to the sharp wit of "The Black Adder," these shows have not only made us laugh but have also become an integral part of British culture. Let's dive into some of the most iconic sitcoms that have shaped the landscape of British television.

Only Fools and Horses: Follow the misadventures of Del Boy and Rodney Trotter, two brothers who are always on the lookout for the next big score. Set in the vibrant borough of Peckham, their get-rich-quick schemes are as endearing as they are doomed to fail. With unforgettable catchphrases and moments that range from uproariously funny to deeply touching, this show is a true classic.

The Black Adder: Travel through different eras of British history with the cunning and sardonic Edmund Blackadder. Each series brings a new generation of the Blackadder family, always accompanied by their loyal but dim-witted servant, Baldrick. From the mediaeval times to the trenches of World War I, the biting humour and brilliant performances have made this series a timeless favourite.

Dad's Army: Set during World War II, this beloved sitcom follows the antics of the Walmington-on-Sea Home Guard. The ragtag group of volunteers, led by the pompous Captain Mainwaring, is determined to defend their town from the impending German invasion. Their bumbling efforts and the camaraderie among the characters provide a perfect blend of humour and nostalgia.

Fawlty Towers: Step into the chaotic world of Basil Fawlty, the eccentric and perpetually frustrated owner of a seaside hotel. With a cast of unforgettable characters, including the ever-patient Polly and the hapless waiter Manuel, this show is a masterclass in farcical comedy. John Cleese's portrayal of Basil's explosive temper and ridiculous schemes has left an indelible mark on television history.

Yes Minister: Delve into the corridors of power with this political satire that brilliantly exposes the absurdities of government bureaucracy. Follow the career of the hapless Jim Hacker as he navigates the treacherous waters of Westminster, aided and often thwarted by the cunning Sir Humphrey Appleby. The show's sharp dialogue and clever plots make it a must-watch for fans of political humour.

Open All Hours: Spend some time in the small corner shop run by the miserly and stuttering Arkwright, along with his long-suffering nephew, Granville. The show's gentle humour and the chemistry between the characters have made it a beloved gem of British television. The day-to-day life of the shop, filled with Arkwright's schemes to save money and Granville's dreams of escape, is both charming and hilarious.

The UK Office: Enter the mundane world of Wernham Hogg, a nondescript paper company in Slough. Ricky Gervais's portrayal of the cringe-inducing boss, David Brent, is both painfully awkward and incredibly funny. The mockumentary style of the show offers a raw and authentic look at office life, with characters that are relatable and moments that are brilliantly uncomfortable.

The Royle Family: Join the Royles in their living room for a slice of everyday British life. This sitcom offers a unique blend of humour and realism, focusing on the interactions of a working-class family. The show's understated comedy and the warmth of its characters make it a standout in the realm of British sitcoms.

And so many more amazing British sitcoms.

So, grab a cup of tea, settle into your comfiest chair, and let's embark on this ultimate British sitcom challenge together!

Contents

Catchphrase Quiz	5
Only Fools and Horses	9
50 Crazy Facts About Only Fools and Horses	9
14 of Del Boy's Funniest One-Liners from Only Fools and Horses	15
The Birth of "Only Fools and Horses"	23
David Jason's Unlikely Casting	23
Iconic British Sitcom Theme Tunes	25
British Humour Compared to Across the Pond	28
Fawlty Towers	32
Questions	32
30 Crazy Facts About "Fawlty Towers"	40
John Cleese: Beyond Fawlty Towers	45
Who Am I? - 20 Questions	51
Clues	51
Ricky Gervais	55
The Making of "The Office" and His Journey to Stardom	55
The Birth of "The Office"	56
David Brent's Cringe-Inducing Quotes and Moments	58
30 Crazy and Bizarre Facts About "The Office"	60
Dad's Army	66
Dad's Army Quiz: 20 Questions	66
The 20 Best "Dad's Army" Moments	72
The Secret History of 'Comedy's Finest Half-Hour'	76
Yes Minister	79
A Hilarious Insight into Inside Politics	79
The Thick of It: The Next Evolution in Political Satire	81
The Black Adder Quiz	84
Questions	84
The Royle Family	92
The Royle Family: A Snapshot of British Working-Class Life	92

Pinwright's Progress	96
The First Sitcom on UK TV: "Pinwright's Progress"	96
Open All Hours	98
The Royle Family Quiz	102
Questions	102
Only Fools and Horses Quiz	108
Questions	108
Peep Show: A Revolutionary British Sitcom	113
Gavin & Stacey: The Charm of Everyday Life	117
Memorable Moments	118
Outnumbered: A Unique Take on Family Life	120
The Black Adder: A Unique Comedy Journey	123
Funniest One-Liners and Gags from "The Black Adder"	125
The Vicar of Dibley: A Heartwarming Comedy	127
Funniest Gags and Moments from "The Vicar of Dibley"	128
Porridge: A Classic British Sitcom	130
Funniest One-Liners and Moments from "Porridge"	131
The Good Life: 10 Crazy and Interesting Facts	133

Catchphrase Quiz

Match the iconic catchphrase to the character and the show it belongs to. Good luck, and no cheating!

- A. Del Boy, Only Fools and Horses
- B. Basil Fawlty, Fawlty Towers
- C. Captain Mainwaring, Dad's Army
- D. Alan Partridge, Alan Partridge
- E. Father Jack, Father Ted
- F. John Cleese, Monty Python's Flying Circus
- G. Sir Humphrey Appleby, Yes Minister
- H. Jez, Peep Show
- I. Baldrick, The Black Adder
- J. Jim Royle, The Royle Family
- K. Various characters, The IT Crowd
- L. Gareth Keenan, The UK Office
- M. Arkwright, Open All Hours
- N. Mrs. Slocombe, Are You Being Served?
- O. Mark Corrigan, Peep Show

1. "Lovely jubbly!"

_____

2. "I have a cunning plan."

_____

3. "Don't tell him, Pike!"

_____

5

4. "Don't mention the war!"

_____

5. "Yes, Minister."

_____

6. "Granville, fetch your cloth!"

_____

7. "I'm the boss. I'm the gaffer."

_____

8. "Smell my cheese!"

_____

9. "This is an ex-parrot!"

_____

10. "Cool. Cool, cool, cool."

_____

11. "That's numberwang!"

_____

12. "I am unanimous in that!"

_____

13. "I'm not a pheasant plucker."

_____

14. "I didn't get where I am today..."

_____

15. "I'm afraid I was very, very drunk."

_____

Answers - Catchphrase Quiz

1. **A. Del Boy, Only Fools and Horses** - "Lovely jubbly!"
2. **I. Baldrick, The Black Adder** - "I have a cunning plan."
3. **C. Captain Mainwaring, Dad's Army** - "Don't tell him, Pike!"
4. **B. Basil Fawlty, Fawlty Towers** - "Don't mention the war!"
5. **G. Sir Humphrey Appleby, Yes Minister** - "Yes, Minister."
6. **M. Arkwright, Open All Hours** - "Granville, fetch your cloth!"
7. **J. Jim Royle, The Royle Family** - "I'm the boss. I'm the gaffer."
8. **D. Alan Partridge, Alan Partridge** - "Smell my cheese!"
9. **F. John Cleese, Monty Python's Flying Circus** - "This is an ex-parrot!"
10. **L. Gareth Keenan, The UK Office** - "Cool. Cool, cool, cool."
11. **K. Various characters, The IT Crowd** - "That's numberwang!"
12. **N. Mrs. Slocombe, Are You Being Served?** - "I am unanimous in that!"
13. **E. Father Jack, Father Ted** - "I'm not a pheasant plucker."
14. **H. Jez, Peep Show** - "I didn't get where I am today..."
15. **O. Mark Corrigan, Peep Show** - "I'm afraid I was very, very drunk."

Did You Know? Catchphrases have been a staple of popular culture for centuries, but have you ever wondered about the origin of the very first known catchphrase? The concept of a catchphrase, a phrase or expression recognized by its repeated and recognizable use, dates back to ancient times.

One of the earliest and most famous catchphrases in history is attributed to Julius Caesar. In 47 BC, after a swift and decisive victory at the Battle of Zela, Caesar reported his success to the Roman Senate with the phrase, "Veni, Vidi, Vici," which translates to "I came, I saw, I conquered." This succinct declaration not only highlighted his military prowess but also became an enduring symbol of triumph and efficiency.

"Veni, Vidi, Vici" has transcended its historical context to become a timeless expression of quick and total victory. Its brevity and impact have made it a favourite reference in various forms of media, including literature, music, and, of course, television. The phrase's enduring popularity demonstrates the power of a well-crafted catchphrase to capture the public's imagination and become embedded in cultural history.

So, when you hear Del Boy from "Only Fools and Horses" exclaim "Lovely jubbly!" you're witnessing the modern-day equivalent of Caesar's triumphant declaration. Just as "Veni, Vidi, Vici" captured the essence of victory in ancient Rome, Del Boy's catchphrase captures the spirit of optimism and success in a more light-hearted and humorous context.

Only Fools and Horses

50 Crazy Facts About Only Fools and Horses

1. **"Lovely Jubbly" Origin**: The phrase "Lovely jubbly," made famous by Del Boy, originally came from an advertisement for Jubbly, a popular orange drink in the 1950s and 1960s.

2. **Longest-Living Sitcom**: "Only Fools and Horses" holds the record as the longest-running British sitcom, with episodes spanning from 1981 to 2003.

3. **Real-Life Market Traders**: David Jason (Del Boy) and Nicholas Lyndhurst (Rodney) spent time with real market traders to prepare for their roles.

4. **The Famous Fall**: The iconic scene where Del Boy falls through the bar was voted the best comedy moment of all time in a 2006 Channel 4 poll.

5. **Original Title**: The show was originally titled "Readies," slang for money, before being changed to "Only Fools and Horses."

6. **Unplanned Popularity**: The show didn't become an instant hit. It gained popularity only after being repeated on television.

7. **Name Origin**: The Trotters' last name is a nod to writer John Sullivan's childhood friend, who was nicknamed "Trotter."

8. **Cameo by the Writer**: John Sullivan, the show's creator, made a cameo appearance in the episode "Little Problems" as a waterbed salesman.

9. **Trigger's Real Name**: Trigger's real name in the show is Colin Ball, though he's rarely called by it.

10. **Del Boy's Income**: According to a study, if Del Boy's various entrepreneurial schemes had been successful, he would have been worth over £6 million.

11. **Rodney's Degrees**: In the episode "If They Could See Us Now," Rodney reveals he has a GCE in Art and Maths, and later gains a Diploma in Computer Science.

12. **Grandad's Funeral**: Lennard Pearce, who played Grandad, passed away during the series, and his character's death was written into the show with a heartfelt tribute episode.

13. **Role Reversal**: Jim Broadbent, who played DCI Roy Slater, was originally considered for the role of Del Boy.

14. **David Jason's Breakthrough**: David Jason was initially known for more serious roles. Del Boy's character transformed his career, making him a household name in comedy.

15. **The Van's Popularity**: The Trotters' yellow Reliant Regal Supervan III is now one of the most recognizable vehicles in British television history.

16. **Cultural Impact**: The show's influence is so significant that it has been referenced in numerous other shows, including "Doctor Who" and "The Vicar of Dibley."

17. **Multiple Christmas Specials**: "Only Fools and Horses" is renowned for its Christmas specials, which became a beloved tradition for UK viewers.

18. **International Versions**: The show was adapted into various international versions, including in the Netherlands ("Toen Was Geluk Heel Gewoon") and Portugal ("O Fura-Vidas").

19. **Marlene and Boycie Spin-off**: The characters Marlene and Boycie were so popular that they got their own spin-off series, "The Green Green Grass."

20. **Auctioned Items**: Items from the show, including Del Boy's flat contents and the iconic yellow van, have been auctioned for thousands of pounds, showcasing the show's lasting legacy and fan dedication.

21. **Injuries on Set**: David Jason (Del Boy) suffered multiple injuries while filming the series, including a dislocated shoulder during the chandelier scene in "A Touch of Glass."

22. **Historical Connection**: The name "Trotter" was inspired by a real-life family John Sullivan knew, adding a touch of authenticity to the characters.

23. **Unscripted Moments**: The famous "Chandelier Scene" in "A Touch of Glass" was filmed in one take, and the actors' reactions were genuine as they had only one chance to get it right.

24. **Pub Naming**: The Nags Head, the pub frequented by the characters, is a real pub name found across the UK, although the show's version was fictional.

25. **Boycie's Laugh**: John Challis, who played Boycie, based his character's distinctive laugh on someone he knew in real life.

26. **Rodney's Nickname**: Rodney's nickname, "Dave," came from Trigger's persistent misnaming, which became a running joke throughout the series.

27. **Delayed Success**: The show wasn't an immediate hit. Its popularity soared after being repeated on BBC1 in 1983.

28. **Real-Life Daughter**: In the episode "A Royal Flush," Del Boy's girlfriend Lisa is played by John Sullivan's real-life daughter, Jo Sullivan.

29. **Cast Bonding**: The cast often socialised outside of filming, with David Jason and Nicholas Lyndhurst forming a close bond similar to their on-screen brotherly relationship.

30. **Grandad's Replacement**: After Lennard Pearce (Grandad) passed away, Buster Merryfield was cast as Uncle Albert. The transition was handled with a respectful and touching storyline.

31. **Iconic Van**: The Trotters' yellow van is actually a 1967 Reliant Regal Supervan III, and several vans were used throughout the series.

32. **Rejection by ITV**: The show was originally pitched to ITV, but they rejected it, a decision they likely regretted given the show's massive success on the BBC.

33. **David Jason's Youth**: David Jason was almost passed over for the role of Del Boy because producers thought he was too old to play a "yuppie" market trader.

34. **Boycie's Catchphrase**: Boycie's famous line, "Marlene!", became so popular that it was often shouted at John Challis in public.

35. **Charity Specials**: The show featured several charity specials, including a crossover with "The Vicar of Dibley" for Comic Relief.

36. **Rodney's Growth**: Over the course of the series, Rodney goes from a naive teenager to a more mature adult, reflecting Nicholas Lyndhurst's own growth as an actor.

37. **Cultural Impact**: The show has influenced British slang, with phrases like "plonker" and "cushty" becoming part of everyday language.

38. **International Fans**: The series has a significant fan base in countries like Australia, New Zealand, and even Serbia, where it was dubbed and became a hit.

39. **Unseen Pilot**: The original pilot episode, which was never broadcast, featured a different actress playing Del Boy's girlfriend.

40. **John Sullivan's Tribute**: The character of Uncle Albert was introduced as a tribute to John Sullivan's own uncle, who had served in the Royal Navy.

41. **Marlene's Dog**: Marlene's dog, Duke, was played by a dog named Paddy, who belonged to the show's animal trainer.

42. **Lost Episode**: A lost episode titled "Licensed to Drill" was discovered in 2011. It was an educational episode about oil drilling, made for schools.

43. **US Remake**: An attempted American remake of "Only Fools and Horses" called "Kings of Van Nuys" was piloted but never made it to series.

44. **Acting Debut**: Gwyneth Strong, who played Cassandra, made her acting debut at the age of 11 in a TV adaptation of "Jane Eyre."

45. **Boycie's Pub**: John Challis, who played Boycie, owns a pub in Shropshire called "The Queen's Arms," which has memorabilia from the show.

46. **Rodney's Education**: Despite Del Boy's constant mockery, Rodney is actually quite well-educated, holding multiple GCEs and a diploma in Computer Science.

47. **No Laugh Track**: Unlike many sitcoms of the era, "Only Fools and Horses" did not use a laugh track, relying instead on live audience reactions.

48. **Lennard Pearce's Audition**: Lennard Pearce, who played Grandad, was the first actor cast in the series after impressing John Sullivan during his audition.

49. **Memorable Props**: The blow-up dolls in "Danger UXD" were filled with helium, causing them to float upwards during filming, which was an unintended but hilarious effect.

50. **John Sullivan's Cameos**: Besides his cameo as a waterbed salesman, John Sullivan appeared in the background of several episodes, blending in with the street scenes.

14 of Del Boy's Funniest One-Liners from Only Fools and Horses

Del Boy, the charismatic wheeler-dealer of "Only Fools and Horses," is known for his quick wit and hilarious one-liners. Here are 14 of his funniest quotes that never fail to bring a smile to our faces:

1. "You can't trust the Old Bill, can ya? Look at that time they planted six gas cookers in my bedroom."

- Del Boy often blames others for his misfortunes. Here, he humorously accuses the police of framing him by planting gas cookers in his room, highlighting his tendency to embellish and deflect blame with a cheeky grin.

2. "You've always been the same, even at school. Nothing but books, learning, education - that's why you're no good at snooker."

- Del Boy frequently teases Rodney for being more academically inclined, contrasting it with his own street smarts. This line is a perfect example of how Del turns Rodney's strengths into perceived weaknesses, in this case, joking that Rodney's focus on education makes him bad at snooker.

3. "Don't worry, Rodney. This time next year, we'll be millionaires!"

- One of Del Boy's most iconic lines, this catchphrase reflects his eternal optimism and ambition. Despite their constant financial struggles, Del is always convinced that their next scheme will finally make them rich.

4. "As Macbeth said to Hamlet in A Midsummer Night's Dream, 'We've been done up like a couple of kippers.'"

- Del Boy hilariously mixes up Shakespearean plays and characters, showcasing his limited literary knowledge while still trying to sound cultured.

5. "They're yuppies. They don't speak proper English like what we do."

- This line highlights Del's disdain for the rising yuppie culture of the 1980s, poking fun at his own working-class roots with his distinct and endearing misuse of grammar.

6. "Asking a Trotter if he knows anything about chandeliers is like asking Mr. Kipling if he knows anything about cakes."

- Del Boy's confidence shines through as he likens his family's expertise to that of a famous cake maker, humorously overstating their knowledge.

7. Rodney: "Del, do they call him Trigger cos he carries a gun?" Del: "No, it's because he looks like a horse."

- This exchange between Rodney and Del about their friend Trigger highlights Del's sharp wit and ability to turn an innocent question into a joke at Trigger's expense.

8. "It's a well-known fact that 90 per cent of all foreign tourists come from abroad."

- Del Boy's mangling of obvious facts into profound-sounding statements is on full display here, making this one of his classic comedic lines.

9. "I am a black belt in origami."

- Del humorously elevates the art of paper folding to the level of a martial art, showcasing his knack for exaggeration.

10. "Rodney, everything between you and I is split straight down the middle: 60-40."

- Del's creative accounting always favours him, even when he insists on fairness, leading to this hilariously skewed split.

11. "It's the toughest chicken I've ever known. It's asked me for a fight in the car park twice."

- Del Boy's hyperbolic description of a tough piece of chicken turns an everyday experience into a laugh-out-loud moment.

12. "I got a Persian rug with more food on it than a menu."

- Del's colourful comparison of a stained rug to a menu full of food options humorously illustrates his dissatisfaction with its condition.

13. "Of course he couldn't swim, he only had one bloody arm. He would have gone around in circles, wouldn't he?"

- Del's blunt assessment of a one-armed man's swimming ability combines dark humour with his characteristic straightforwardness.

14. "Not only have you managed to sink every battleship and aircraft carrier that you've ever sailed on, but now you've gone and knackered a gravy boat."

- In this line, Del Boy humorously exaggerates Rodney's clumsiness, comparing it to major naval disasters and then bringing it down to the domestic level of ruining a gravy boat.

The Dream of Becoming Millionaires in "Only Fools and Horses"

One of the most iconic and recurring catchphrases in "Only Fools and Horses" is Del Boy's optimistic declaration, "This time next year, we'll be millionaires!" This line encapsulates the heart and soul of the series and provides insight into Del Boy's character and the show's themes.

Del Boy, played by David Jason, is the quintessential wheeler-dealer, always involved in one get-rich-quick scheme after another. Despite the numerous failures and setbacks he faces, Del Boy never loses hope. His optimism is boundless, and he genuinely believes that his next business venture will be the one that makes him and his brother Rodney millionaires. This unwavering belief in a better future is a core aspect of his character and a driving force in the series.

The Trotter family, consisting of Del Boy, his younger brother Rodney (Nicholas Lyndhurst), and their elderly grandfather (and later Uncle Albert), live in a council flat in Peckham, South London. They are constantly struggling to make ends meet, and their lives are a series of ups and downs. Del Boy's catchphrase is a reflection of their aspirations and dreams to escape their financial difficulties and improve their social standing. It resonates with many viewers who can relate to the desire for a better life.

The catchphrase is also a source of humor and irony. Del Boy's schemes are often outlandish and doomed to fail, making his confidence in them all the more amusing. The audience is in on the joke, knowing that despite his grand plans, things are likely to go hilariously wrong. This creates a comedic tension that is a hallmark of the show.

Beyond the humor, the catchphrase symbolizes hope and resilience. No matter how many times Del Boy and Rodney fail, they always get back up and try again. This resilience is inspiring and adds depth to the characters. It shows that they are not just foolish dreamers but also hardworking individuals who refuse to give up on their dreams.

"Only Fools and Horses" aired during a time of significant economic change in the UK. The show began in the early 1980s, a period marked by economic hardship for many working-class families. Del Boy's aspiration to become a millionaire reflects the aspirations of many during that time. It captures the spirit of entrepreneurship and the belief that anyone can achieve success with enough hard work and a bit of luck.

Interestingly, the show eventually fulfills Del Boy's dream in the 1996 Christmas special "Time on Our Hands." The Trotters find an antique watch in their garage that sells at auction for millions of pounds. This moment is both satisfying and poignant, as it rewards the characters for their perseverance and hard work. It also brings the series full circle, giving fans a sense of closure while maintaining the humor and charm that made the show beloved.

Del Boy's catchphrase, "This time next year, we'll be millionaires!" is more than just a recurring line; it is a cornerstone of "Only Fools and Horses." It embodies the show's themes of hope, resilience, and the pursuit of a better life, while also providing humor and a touch of irony. Through this catchphrase, the series captures the hearts of its audience, making it one of the most cherished sitcoms in British television history.

Character Evolution and Development in "Only Fools and Horses"

Del Boy

Del Boy, portrayed by David Jason, begins the series as a charming but unscrupulous market trader, always on the lookout for the next big score. Throughout the series, Del's character matures significantly. Initially driven by his get-rich-quick schemes and flamboyant personality, Del slowly reveals a more vulnerable side, showing deep loyalty and love for his family. His dream of becoming a millionaire, while often humorous in its futility, underscores his relentless optimism and resilience. Del's relationship with Rodney evolves from that of a domineering elder brother to a more equal partnership, marked by mutual respect and understanding. This growth adds depth to Del's character, making him one of the most beloved figures in British television.

Rodney

Rodney, played by Nicholas Lyndhurst, starts as the naive and idealistic younger brother, often the butt of Del's jokes and schemes. Over the years, Rodney grows from a somewhat hapless youth into a more assertive and confident individual. His pursuit of education and various career aspirations highlight his desire to break free from the family's cycle of poverty. Rodney's relationship with Del is central to his development; despite their frequent bickering, their bond is unbreakable. Rodney's marriage to Cassandra also plays a significant role in his maturation, as he navigates the complexities of adult life and responsibility. His evolution from a "plonker" to a more grounded character is both touching and relatable.

Grandad

Lennard Pearce's Grandad serves as the Trotter family's elder statesman in the early seasons. He is a source of wisdom, albeit often delivered with a comedic touch. Grandad's character provides a link to the past, grounding Del and Rodney with tales of bygone days and family history. His relationship with his grandsons is affectionate and supportive, despite his frequent misunderstandings and bumbling nature. Grandad's passing was a pivotal moment in the series, leading to heartfelt tributes and a deeper exploration of family dynamics and loss, showcasing the show's ability to blend comedy with poignant, real-life issues.

Uncle Albert

Introduced after Grandad's death, Uncle Albert, played by Buster Merryfield, becomes an integral part of the Trotter family. With his memorable "During the war..." anecdotes, Albert provides comic relief while also serving as a father figure. His arrival brings a fresh dynamic to the Trotter household, often acting as a mediator between Del and Rodney. Albert's own backstory as a sailor and his life experiences add richness to the family narrative. Over time, his character reveals a profound sense of loyalty and courage, particularly in the face of personal hardships, reinforcing the show's themes of resilience and family unity.

The interactions between Del Boy, Rodney, Grandad, and Uncle Albert form the heart of "Only Fools and Horses." Their relationships are characterized by a mix of humor, conflict, and deep affection, reflecting the complexities of real-life family dynamics. Del's relentless schemes, Rodney's quest for a better life, Grandad's nostalgic stories, and Albert's war tales create a tapestry of interwoven narratives that resonate with viewers. The show's ability to balance comedy with moments of genuine emotion allows the characters to grow in meaningful ways, endearing them to audiences and ensuring the series' lasting popularity. Through their personal growth and evolving relationships, these characters highlight the importance of family, hope, and perseverance, making "Only Fools and Horses" a timeless classic.

Behind-the-Scenes Stories and Production Secrets of "Only Fools and Horses"

The Chandelier Scene: One Take Wonder

One of the most iconic moments in "Only Fools and Horses" is the chandelier scene from the episode "A Touch of Glass." The scene where Del Boy and Rodney accidentally drop a priceless chandelier was meticulously planned and executed in a single take. The production team had only one chance to get it right because they could not afford to break more than one chandelier. The tension was palpable on set as everyone knew the stakes. David Jason and Nicholas Lyndhurst delivered their lines with perfect timing, and the crew held their breath as the chandelier came crashing down. The actors' stunned reactions were genuine, capturing the disbelief and horror that made the scene so memorable. This behind-the-scenes gamble paid off spectacularly, creating a moment that would be celebrated as one of the greatest in British comedy.

Lennard Pearce's Legacy: A Heartfelt Tribute

The sudden death of Lennard Pearce, who played Grandad, was a significant and emotional challenge for the cast and crew. Lennard passed away during the filming of the fourth series, leaving a void that was deeply felt by everyone involved. The decision to address his passing within the show was handled with great sensitivity. In the episode "Strained Relations," Grandad's death is poignantly addressed, with the Trotter family grappling with their loss. The scenes were shot with real emotion, as the grief portrayed by the actors was heartfelt. Introducing Buster Merryfield as Uncle Albert helped the show transition through this difficult period. Albert's character brought new life and humor to the series, but the legacy of Lennard Pearce was always honored and remembered fondly by the cast and crew, highlighting the deep bonds formed during production.

The Blow-Up Dolls Incident: A Hilarious Mishap

In the episode "Danger UXD," Del Boy and Rodney inadvertently come into possession of a batch of blow-up dolls. What was intended to be a simple comedic prop turned into an unexpected behind-the-scenes challenge. The dolls were filled with helium to make them appear lifelike, but during the filming, they began to float upwards uncontrollably. This unplanned hilarity added an extra layer of chaos to the scene, with cast members struggling to keep straight faces as they wrangled the rogue dolls. The crew had to quickly adapt to the situation, and the actors improvised brilliantly, turning a potential mishap into a comedy goldmine. The incident showcased the spontaneous and flexible nature of the production team, proving that sometimes the funniest moments come from the most unexpected situations.

The Birth of "Only Fools and Horses"

The creation of "Only Fools and Horses" itself is a fascinating story. John Sullivan, the show's creator, drew heavily from his own experiences growing up in a working-class family in London. Sullivan had a deep understanding of the characters he was writing about, which is why they resonated so well with the audience. Initially, the BBC was hesitant to greenlight the series. It was only after persistent lobbying from Sullivan and a successful pilot that the show was picked up. The original title was "Readies," a slang term for money, but it was changed to "Only Fools and Horses" based on a saying Sullivan had come across: "Only fools and horses work for a living." This title perfectly encapsulated the ethos of the Trotters and their perpetual quest for easy money.

David Jason's Unlikely Casting

David Jason, who would become synonymous with the character of Del Boy, was not the first choice for the role. The producers originally considered Jim Broadbent, who would later play DCI Roy Slater in the series, for the part. However, David Jason's audition was so compelling that he ultimately won the role. Interestingly, Jason was primarily known for his work in drama and was not immediately seen as a fit for a comedic lead. His versatility and ability to infuse Del Boy with a mix of charm, bravado, and vulnerability proved to be a masterstroke. Jason's portrayal of Del Boy transformed his career and became one of the most beloved characters in British television history. His chemistry with Nicholas Lyndhurst was also key to the show's success, turning what could have been a simple comedy into a richly layered, character-driven series.

The Real-Life Market Experience

To ensure authenticity in their portrayal of market traders, David Jason and Nicholas Lyndhurst spent time with real market traders in London. This hands-on research helped them understand the nuances of the trade and the lifestyle of their characters. Jason and Lyndhurst observed the traders' banter, their sales techniques, and their unique ways of interacting with customers. This experience translated into their performances, adding a layer of realism to their roles. The actors' dedication to embodying the Trotter brothers as genuine market traders contributed significantly to the show's credibility and charm. Their ability to capture the essence of these traders was evident in every scene, grounding the often outlandish plots in a believable world.

Iconic British Sitcom Theme Tunes

The Black Adder

"The Black Adder" theme tune, composed by Howard Goodall, is a grand and humorous orchestral piece that evolves with each series. The original series features a medieval-style fanfare, reflecting the historical setting. As the series progresses through different eras, the theme tune adapts, maintaining its core melody but incorporating elements reflective of the respective periods, such as Elizabethan, Regency, and World War I. This clever musical evolution mirrors the show's time-traveling narrative, making the theme tune an integral part of its storytelling.

Dad's Army

"Dad's Army" is set to the tune of "Who Do You Think You Are Kidding, Mr. Hitler?", a song written by Jimmy Perry and Derek Taverner, and performed by wartime entertainer Bud Flanagan. The song's nostalgic, 1940s-style composition perfectly matches the show's setting during World War II. It captures the spirit of the Home Guard with its patriotic yet playful tone. The lyrics humorously undermine Hitler's threat, setting the stage for the show's light-hearted yet respectful depiction of wartime Britain.

Fawlty Towers

The theme tune of "Fawlty Towers" is an instrumental piece composed by Dennis Wilson. Its gentle, classical style, featuring a solo piano, contrasts sharply with the chaos and farcical humor of the show, creating an ironic juxtaposition. This serene music underscores the absurdity of Basil Fawlty's manic world, making the tranquility of the theme all the more humorous. The simplicity and elegance of the tune add to its charm, making it an unforgettable part of the series.

Only Fools and Horses

The theme tune of "Only Fools and Horses" is one of the most recognizable in British television history. Written and sung by the show's creator, John Sullivan, the lyrics reflect the Trotters' perpetual struggle and optimism. The catchy, upbeat melody with lines like "No income tax, no VAT" perfectly encapsulates the essence of Del Boy's wheeler-dealer persona. The theme tune's unique charm lies in its ability to immediately evoke the world of the Trotters, setting the tone for the comedic yet heartfelt stories to follow.

Yes Minister

The theme tune for "Yes Minister" and its sequel "Yes, Prime Minister" was composed by Ronnie Hazlehurst. The jaunty, upbeat melody is played by a solo clarinet, with an undercurrent of British pomp and circumstance. The music complements the show's satirical look at British politics, embodying the clever, witty, and somewhat whimsical nature of the series. The light-hearted tune belies the sharp political satire within, making it an iconic piece of television music.

Open All Hours

The theme tune for "Open All Hours," composed by Joseph Ascher, is a nostalgic piece that evokes a sense of timeless British small-town life. The gentle, whimsical melody reflects the quirky yet endearing nature of the show, capturing the essence of Arkwright's small shop and its eccentric customers. The music's simplicity and charm perfectly align with the show's setting, making it a memorable and fitting accompaniment to the series.

The UK Office

The theme tune for "The UK Office" is "Handbags and Gladrags," originally written by Mike d'Abo. Over the years, this poignant song has been performed by various artists, including Rod Stewart and Stereophonics, each bringing their unique style to the timeless melody. The version used in the show, arranged by Big George, features a melancholy and reflective tone that starkly contrasts with the often uncomfortable and comedic situations depicted in the series.

"Handbags and Gladrags" underscores the mundane reality of office life, adding an emotional depth that complements the show's mockumentary style. The song's lyrics, such as "Once I was a young man / And all I thought I had to do was smile," resonate with the themes of unfulfilled aspirations and the passage of time, mirroring the lives of the office workers in Wernham Hogg. This reflective quality adds a layer of introspection to the series, highlighting the characters' struggles and dreams amidst the daily grind. The choice of this song elevates the show's narrative, making it not just a comedic portrayal of office life, but a deeper exploration of the human condition.

The Royle Family

The theme tune for "The Royle Family" is "Half the World Away" by Oasis. The song's wistful lyrics and gentle melody perfectly reflect the show's focus on the ordinary yet profound moments of family life. Oasis, known for their working-class roots and anthems of everyday struggle and resilience, provided a fitting soundtrack for the series. The choice of this song adds a layer of sentimentality and warmth, making it a perfect match for the show's setting in a working-class home.

"Half the World Away" resonates deeply with the themes of "The Royle Family." The song captures the essence of longing and the bittersweet passage of time, much like the series itself, which beautifully portrays the simplicity and complexity of family life. Both Oasis and the Royles share a connection to their working-class upbringing, emphasizing love, humor, and the unvarnished reality of their lives. The music and the series together celebrate the unpretentious, genuine moments that define a family's bond, making the theme tune not just an introduction, but an integral part of the show's emotional tapestry.

Keeping Up Appearances

"Keeping Up Appearances" features a jaunty, upbeat theme composed by Nick Ingman. The lively tune matches the show's comedic tone and the social-climbing antics of Hyacinth Bucket (pronounced "Bouquet"). The music's playful nature reflects Hyacinth's pretentiousness and the show's light-hearted critique of social pretensions.

Are You Being Served?

The theme tune for "Are You Being Served?" was composed by Ronnie Hazlehurst and features a blend of orchestral music with store announcements, creating the atmosphere of a bustling department store. The whimsical and catchy tune perfectly sets the stage for the show's retail-based comedy, making it instantly recognizable and beloved by fans.

Absolutely Fabulous

The theme tune for "Absolutely Fabulous" is "This Wheel's on Fire," performed by Julie Driscoll and Adrian Edmondson. The song's psychedelic rock style complements the show's outrageous humor and the flamboyant lifestyles of its main characters, Edina and Patsy. The choice of music reflects the show's irreverent and fashionable spirit, making it a standout theme in British sitcoms.

British Humour Compared to Across the Pond

British humour is renowned for its wit, subtlety, and often self-deprecating nature. It thrives on irony, sarcasm, and the ability to find humour in everyday situations. This style of comedy often relies on wordplay and clever dialogue rather than physical gags or slapstick. Shows like "Fawlty Towers" and "Yes Minister" exemplify this with their sharp, intelligent scripts that require viewers to pay close attention to fully appreciate the jokes. The understated delivery and dry wit that characterise British humour can be traced back to the country's literary and theatrical traditions, where clever dialogue and social commentary have always played a significant role.

In contrast, American humour tends to be more direct and overt. While it also values witty dialogue, American comedy often leans more heavily on physical humour, sight gags, and situational comedy. Shows like "Friends" and "Seinfeld" are great examples of this, with their focus on humorous situations and character interactions that are immediately accessible and visually engaging. American humour also tends to be more optimistic and energetic, reflecting the broader cultural emphasis on positivity and resilience.

One key difference is the British tendency to embrace darker, more cynical themes in their humour. British comedies often highlight the absurdities and frustrations of everyday life, with characters who are flawed and relatable. This can be seen in shows like "The Office" (UK) and "The Royle Family," where the humour often stems from the mundanity and sometimes bleak aspects of life. This contrasts with the more aspirational and upbeat tone often found in American sitcoms, where characters frequently strive for and achieve personal growth and success.

Another aspect of British humour is its use of social and class commentary. Many British comedies, such as "Only Fools and Horses" and "Keeping Up Appearances," derive much of their humour from the social dynamics and class distinctions within British society. This type of humour can be quite specific to the British experience, making it unique but sometimes harder to translate for international audiences. American comedies, while they do address social issues, tend to focus more on individual character arcs and personal relationships.

British humour also tends to be more self-deprecating. Characters in British comedies often poke fun at themselves and their shortcomings, which can endear them to the audience. This self-awareness and willingness to embrace imperfection is a hallmark of British comedy and contrasts with the often more polished and confident characters found in American sitcoms. This difference can be seen in the character of David Brent in "The Office" (UK) compared to Michael Scott in the American version of the show.

"The IT Crowd"

The American version of "The IT Crowd" was a near shot-for-shot remake of the British original. However, despite featuring Richard Ayoade reprising his role as Moss, the pilot was not picked up. The humour, which heavily relied on British cultural references and a specific type of awkwardness, did not translate well to an American audience, leading to its quick cancellation.

"Coupling"

Known as the British "Friends," "Coupling" was a racy and witty comedy that delved into the relationships and sexual escapades of six friends. The American version tried to replicate the success by closely mirroring the British scripts but fell flat. The cultural differences in humour, particularly regarding the frankness about sex, did not resonate with American viewers, and the show was cancelled after just a few episodes.

"Red Dwarf"

The sci-fi comedy "Red Dwarf" enjoyed massive success in the UK but struggled in its American adaptation. Despite several attempts to recreate the show for a U.S. audience, none managed to capture the original's quirky charm and dark humour. The pilot episodes were not well-received, and the projects were ultimately abandoned.

"Fawlty Towers"

"Fawlty Towers" has seen multiple attempts to adapt it for American audiences, with shows like "Amanda's" and "Payne." However, the biting wit and farcical situations, so perfectly executed by John Cleese, did not translate well. The essence of Basil Fawlty's character and the show's unique brand of humour proved too challenging to adapt, resulting in short-lived runs.

"The Inbetweeners"

The American version of "The Inbetweeners" struggled to capture the raw, often crude humour that made the British original so popular. The characters' interactions, heavily influenced by British teenage culture, did not resonate with American viewers in the same way. The show was cancelled after one season due to poor ratings and reviews.

Fawlty Towers

Questions

1. **What is the name of the hotel owned by Basil Fawlty?**

    A. The Grand Hotel
    B. Fawlty Towers
    C. The Majestic
    D. Seaside Inn

2. **What is the name of Basil Fawlty's wife?**

    A. Polly
    B. Sybil
    C. Mary
    D. Sarah

3. **Who is the Spanish waiter at Fawlty Towers?**

    A. Manuel
    B. Pablo
    C. Juan
    D. Carlos

4. **In which English town is Fawlty Towers set?**

    A. London
    B. Bath
    C. Torquay
    D. Brighton

5. **What is Basil Fawlty's catchphrase when he's frustrated?**

    A. "Oh, bother!"
    B. "What is it now?"
    C. "Right, that's it!"
    D. "I'm terribly sorry!"

6. Which actor played the role of Basil Fawlty?

   A. Rowan Atkinson
   B. Stephen Fry J
   C. David Jason
   D. John Cleese

7. What is the name of the maid who works at Fawlty Towers?

   A. Polly
   B. Daisy
   C. Lucy
   D. Jane

8. What is the main reason Basil is always annoyed with Manuel?

   A. He steals from the hotel
   B. He can't speak English well
   C. He is always late
   D. He flirts with Sybil

9. Which war does Basil often mention inappropriately?

   A. World War I
   B. The Boer War
   C. World War II
   D. The Falklands War

10. What type of business is Fawlty Towers?

    A. Bed and Breakfast
    B. Guest House
    C. Boutique Hotel
    D. Resort

11. In the episode "The Germans," what does the sign outside the hotel read after being mischievously altered?

    A. Warty Towels
    B. Farty Towels
    C. Fawlty Powers
    D. Flowery Twats

12. Who is the Major, a regular guest at the hotel?

    A. Major Thomas
    B. Major Smith
    C. Major Gowen
    D. Major Anderson

13. What kind of pet does Basil have a particular dislike for?

    A. Cats
    B. Dogs
    C. Birds
    D. Hamsters

14. In the episode "The Kipper and the Corpse," what causes the guest to die?

    A. Food poisoning
    B. Heart attack
    C. Allergic reaction
    D. Choking

15. Which famous comedian co-wrote "Fawlty Towers" with John Cleese?

    A. Michael Palin
    B. Eric Idle
    C. Graham Chapman
    D. Connie Booth

16. What does Basil famously injure in the episode "Gourmet Night"?

    A. His back
    B. His leg
    C. His arm
    D. His head

17. What type of cuisine is being served in the episode "Gourmet Night"?

    A. Italian

        B. French
        C. Indian
        D. Greek

18. In the episode "Communication Problems," what is Mrs. Richards' main complaint?

        A. The food
        B. The noise
        C. The view
        D. The staff

19. How many episodes of "Fawlty Towers" were made?

        A. 12
        B. 20
        C. 24
        D. 30

20. In the episode "The Hotel Inspectors," how does Basil try to identify the inspectors?

        A. By their clothes
        B. By their mannerisms
        C. By their luggage
        D. By their accents

Fawlty Towers Quiz - Answers

1. What is the name of the hotel owned by Basil Fawlty?

- **B. Fawlty Towers** - *Fawlty Towers* is the titular hotel run by the irascible Basil Fawlty. The name is a play on words, as "faulty" describes the often chaotic and dysfunctional nature of the establishment.

2. What is the name of Basil Fawlty's wife?

- **B. Sybil** - Sybil Fawlty, played by Prunella Scales, is Basil's wife and often the voice of reason. She is known for her distinctive laugh and no-nonsense attitude.

3. Who is the Spanish waiter at Fawlty Towers?

- **Manuel** - Manuel, played by Andrew Sachs, is the well-meaning but linguistically challenged waiter from Barcelona. His misunderstandings are a frequent source of comedy.

4. In which English town is Fawlty Towers set?

- **C. Torquay** - The show is set in the seaside town of Torquay in Devon. The location was inspired by John Cleese's stay at a real hotel in the town.

5. What is Basil Fawlty's catchphrase when he's frustrated?

- **C. "Right, that's it!"** - Basil often uses this phrase when he reaches the end of his patience, usually just before launching into a tirade.

6. Which actor played the role of Basil Fawlty?

- **John Cleese** - John Cleese, a member of the Monty Python comedy group, created and starred as the iconic character Basil Fawlty.

7. What is the name of the maid who works at Fawlty Towers?

- **Polly** - Polly Sherman, played by Connie Booth, is the maid and waitress who often has to help Basil out of difficult situations. She is also co-writer of the show with Cleese.

8. What is the main reason Basil is always annoyed with Manuel?

- **B. He can't speak English well** - Manuel's limited English skills lead to many comical misunderstandings, much to Basil's frustration.

9. Which war does Basil often mention inappropriately?

- **C. World War II** - Basil frequently and inappropriately references World War II, most famously in the episode "The Germans" where he says, "Don't mention the war!"

10. What type of business is Fawlty Towers?

- **B. Guest House** - Fawlty Towers is a small guest house, though Basil's pretensions often lead him to behave as if he is running a grand hotel.

11. In the episode "The Germans," what does the sign outside the hotel read after being mischievously altered?

- **B. Farty Towels** - In "The Germans," the sign is changed to "Farty Towels," one of several humorous alterations seen throughout the series.

12. Who is the Major, a regular guest at the hotel?

- **C. Major Gowen** - Major Gowen, played by Ballard Berkeley, is a somewhat senile and eccentric permanent resident of Fawlty Towers.

13. What kind of pet does Basil have a particular dislike for?

- **B. Dogs** - Basil has a particular disdain for dogs, as seen in episodes like "The Kipper and the Corpse" where a guest's dog is involved in a mix-up.

14. In the episode "The Kipper and the Corpse," what causes the guest to die?

- **B. Heart attack** - The guest dies of a heart attack, but Basil mistakenly thinks it might be the kippers (smoked fish) he served.

15. Which famous comedian co-wrote "Fawlty Towers" with John Cleese?

- **Connie Booth** - Connie Booth, who also played Polly, co-wrote the series with John Cleese. They were married at the time of the first series.

16. What does Basil famously injure in the episode "Gourmet Night"?

- **B. His leg** - Basil injures his leg, leading to the famous scene where he gets frustrated with his car and starts hitting it with a tree branch.

17. What type of cuisine is being served in the episode "Gourmet Night"?

- **B. French** - "Gourmet Night" features a French cuisine night that goes disastrously wrong, including a memorable scene with a duck being served instead of a main course.

18. In the episode "Communication Problems," what is Mrs. Richards' main complaint?

- **B. The noise** - Mrs. Richards, a hard-of-hearing and difficult guest, complains incessantly about the noise and various other issues.

19. How many episodes of "Fawlty Towers" were made?

- **A. 12** - Only 12 episodes of "Fawlty Towers" were made, spread across two series. Despite the limited number of episodes, the show remains a timeless classic.

20. In the episode "The Hotel Inspectors," how does Basil try to identify the inspectors?

- **B. By their mannerisms** - Basil attempts to identify the hotel inspectors by their mannerisms, leading to a series of hilarious misunderstandings and escalating chaos.

Why Only 12 Episodes

"Fawlty Towers," despite its immense popularity and critical acclaim, only produced 12 episodes over two series. One of the primary reasons for this limited run was the perfectionist nature of its creators, John Cleese and Connie Booth. Both Cleese and Booth were determined to maintain a high standard of writing and performance, ensuring that each episode was meticulously crafted and packed with quality humour and storytelling. They believed that extending the series too far might dilute its comedic impact and lead to a decline in quality. By keeping the episode count low, they were able to focus intensely on each script, refining the dialogue, characters, and situations to create a near-flawless comedy experience.

Another reason for the brief run was the intense effort required to produce each episode. Writing and filming "Fawlty Towers" was a demanding process, often leading to long hours and significant stress for everyone involved. John Cleese, in particular, was heavily involved in both the writing and the performance, striving to achieve the comedic timing and physical humour that made the show so special. The rigorous nature of the production meant that sustaining such a high level of effort over more episodes was not feasible without compromising the health and well-being of the cast and crew. Cleese and Booth preferred to end the series on a high note rather than risking burnout and a potential drop in the show's exceptional standards.

Lastly, both Cleese and Booth had other professional and personal commitments that influenced their decision to keep "Fawlty Towers" concise. John Cleese was still involved with Monty Python and had numerous other projects, while Connie Booth pursued various acting and writing opportunities. Additionally, their personal relationship, having been married and then divorced during the show's run, added another layer of complexity. Maintaining a collaborative creative partnership after their separation was challenging, and they chose to preserve their professional integrity and the show's legacy by concluding it with a short but impactful run. This decision ultimately contributed to "Fawlty Towers" becoming a timeless classic, remembered for its brilliant writing, unforgettable characters, and its perfect, albeit brief, contribution to television comedy.

30 Crazy Facts About "Fawlty Towers"

1. **Real Inspiration**: The character of Basil Fawlty was inspired by a real hotel owner named Donald Sinclair, whom John Cleese encountered while staying at the Gleneagles Hotel in Torquay.
2. **Hotel Exterior**: The exterior shots of Fawlty Towers were actually of a country house hotel called Wooburn Grange Country Club in Buckinghamshire, which was later destroyed by fire.
3. **Connie Booth's Dual Role**: Connie Booth not only co-wrote the series with John Cleese but also starred as Polly, showcasing her versatility.
4. **First Episode Misfire**: The first episode, "A Touch of Class," was almost not broadcast because the BBC executives did not find it funny. It was later aired after Cleese and Booth insisted.
5. **No Laughter Track**: Unlike many sitcoms of the time, "Fawlty Towers" was filmed with a live studio audience, ensuring genuine laughter in response to the antics on screen.
6. **Manual's Accent**: Andrew Sachs, who played Manuel, was actually German-born. He mastered the Spanish accent for his role, which many viewers believed was authentic.

40

7. **Physical Comedy Injuries**: John Cleese sustained several minor injuries during filming due to the physical comedy required, particularly in scenes where he loses his temper.
8. **Connie Booth's Post-Show Career**: After "Fawlty Towers," Connie Booth retired from acting and became a psychotherapist in London.
9. **Prunella Scales' Audition**: Prunella Scales originally auditioned for a different role but was cast as Sybil after impressing the producers with her comedic timing.
10. **Andrew Sachs' Real-Life Injury**: Sachs was accidentally injured during the filming of the episode "The Germans" when Cleese hit him with a frying pan. Sachs was badly burned, leading to him suing the production for damages.
11. **Major Gowen's Last Role**: Ballard Berkeley, who played Major Gowen, continued acting into his late 80s. "Fawlty Towers" was one of his last major roles.
12. **Sybil's Hair**: Prunella Scales wore a wig throughout the series to create Sybil's distinctive hairstyle.
13. **Manual's Pet Rat**: In the episode "Basil the Rat," Manuel's pet "Siberian Hamster" was actually played by a real rat named Basil.
14. **Script Perfection**: John Cleese and Connie Booth wrote each script over many months, often perfecting the dialogue down to the last word, which contributed to the show's high quality.
15. **Cultural Impact**: "Fawlty Towers" was named the best British TV series of all time by the British Film Institute in 2000.
16. **Recurring Joke**: The sign outside Fawlty Towers is changed in almost every episode, often with humorous and inappropriate anagrams like "Fatty Owls" and "Watery Fowls."
17. **Richard Ingrams as a Guest Star**: Richard Ingrams, the editor of the satirical magazine Private Eye, guest-starred as the guest who dies in "The Kipper and the Corpse."

18. **German Criticism**: The episode "The Germans" faced criticism from German viewers but also received praise for its bold humour and satirical take on British attitudes towards Germans.
19. **John Cleese's Height**: John Cleese's towering height (6'5") was used to great comedic effect, particularly in scenes with the much shorter Andrew Sachs.
20. **Only One Director**: All 12 episodes were directed by Bob Spiers, ensuring a consistent tone and style throughout the series.
21. **Length of Episodes**: Each episode of "Fawlty Towers" was originally 30 minutes long, with tight, well-crafted storylines that left no room for filler content.
22. **Multi-Camera Setup**: The show was filmed using a multi-camera setup, a technique not as commonly used for British sitcoms at the time, which helped capture the dynamic physical comedy.
23. **Cleese's Decision to End the Show**: John Cleese decided to end the series after just 12 episodes to avoid running out of ideas and maintaining the show's high standards.
24. **Basil's Explosive Temper**: Cleese modeled Basil Fawlty's outbursts on his own father's temper, which he used to great comedic effect.
25. **Guest Stars**: The show featured many guest stars who went on to become well-known actors, including Una Stubbs, who played Alice in the episode "The Anniversary."
26. **Continuity Errors**: Despite its meticulous writing, the show has several continuity errors, such as the ever-changing layout of the hotel and inconsistent character backstories.
27. **Original Broadcast**: When first broadcast in 1975, "Fawlty Towers" did not initially achieve high ratings but later gained popularity through repeats.
28. **Sybil's Nickname for Basil**: Sybil often calls Basil "Basil the Rat" in a nod to the title of the episode featuring Manuel's pet rat, showcasing their combative relationship.

29. **Language Barrier**: Manuel's catchphrase, "Que?", meaning "What?" in Spanish, became iconic and is still recognized as a hallmark of the character's confusion.
30. **Modern Adaptations**: "Fawlty Towers" has inspired numerous adaptations and spin-offs worldwide, including an American pilot that never aired. Despite the many attempts, none have captured the unique charm and success of the original.

Behind-the-Scenes Stories and Production Secrets of "Fawlty Towers"

The Real Basil Fawlty: Donald Sinclair's Legacy

The character of Basil Fawlty, brought to life by John Cleese, was inspired by a real hotel owner named Donald Sinclair. Cleese encountered Sinclair when the Monty Python team stayed at the Gleneagles Hotel in Torquay. Sinclair's eccentric and rude behavior became the blueprint for Basil. Sinclair's antics included throwing Eric Idle's briefcase out of a window because he thought it might contain a bomb, and chastising Terry Gilliam for not holding his fork correctly. Cleese found Sinclair's outrageous mannerisms so fascinating that he knew he had to base a character on him. This real-life inspiration added a layer of authenticity and absurdity to Basil Fawlty, making him one of the most memorable characters in television history.

Prunella Scales' Audition and Sybil's Iconic Laugh

Prunella Scales wasn't the initial choice for Sybil Fawlty. In fact, Joan Sanderson, who later guest-starred on the show, was considered for the role. However, during her audition, Scales delivered an impressive performance that immediately caught the attention of John Cleese and the producers. Scales' ability to combine a no-nonsense attitude with sharp comedic timing made her perfect for the role. To create Sybil's signature look, Scales wore a wig, which became a defining feature of her character. Sybil's high-pitched, mocking laugh, often directed at Basil's misfortunes, became one of the show's most recognizable elements. This laugh wasn't scripted; it was Scales' natural response to the character, adding a unique touch that further solidified Sybil as a beloved figure in the series.

Manuel's Real-Life Injuries and Dedication

Andrew Sachs, who played the lovable but hapless Spanish waiter Manuel, was dedicated to his role to the point of enduring physical pain. During the filming of the episode "The Germans," there was a scene where John Cleese's character, Basil, hits Manuel over the head with a frying pan. Due to a miscalculation, Sachs ended up with second-degree burns from a hot pan, leading to a short hospitalization. Despite this, Sachs continued filming, showcasing his commitment and professionalism. This incident is a testament to the physical comedy that "Fawlty Towers" often required. Sachs' portrayal of Manuel, with his earnest attempts to understand English and his constant bewilderment, brought warmth and humor to the show, making him a fan favorite.

The Unscripted Genius of the Car Thrashing Scene

One of the most iconic scenes in "Fawlty Towers" involves Basil Fawlty taking out his frustration on his car by thrashing it with a tree branch. This moment of pure comedic gold occurred in the episode "Gourmet Night." The scene was not originally scripted to be as intense as it turned out. Cleese, known for his towering height and expressive physicality, improvised much of the sequence. His genuine frustration and exaggerated movements, combined with the absurdity of attacking a car with a branch, made the scene unforgettable. The spontaneity of Cleese's performance and the genuine reactions from the crew, who were trying not to laugh, added to the authenticity and hilarity of the moment.

The Collaboration of John Cleese and Connie Booth

John Cleese and Connie Booth, who played Polly Sherman, were not only co-stars but also co-writers of "Fawlty Towers." Their real-life relationship, which included marriage and later divorce, influenced their collaborative process. Despite their personal challenges, Cleese and Booth maintained a professional partnership that was instrumental in creating the show's unique humor. Booth's role as Polly, the pragmatic and resourceful maid, often balanced Basil's chaotic energy. Their writing sessions were intense and meticulous, often taking several months to perfect a single script. This dedication to quality over quantity ensured that each episode was packed with sharp wit and memorable moments, contributing to the show's enduring legacy.

The Unexpected Success of the "Rat" Episode

The final episode of "Fawlty Towers," titled "Basil the Rat," features a subplot where Manuel's pet "Siberian Hamster" is discovered to be a rat. This storyline added an extra layer of chaos as the hotel was undergoing a health inspection. The rat, affectionately named Basil, became an unexpected star of the episode. The production team had to ensure the rat was handled safely, and several takes were required to get the scenes just right. The episode showcased the series' ability to blend farcical elements with sharp dialogue and character interactions. The unexpected success of this episode, with its mix of slapstick and situational comedy, epitomized what made "Fawlty Towers" a classic: the perfect combination of well-crafted scripts, stellar performances, and unpredictable humor.

John Cleese: Beyond Fawlty Towers

John Cleese is a towering figure in the world of comedy, renowned for his sharp wit, impeccable timing, and groundbreaking contributions to the genre. While "Fawlty Towers" remains one of his most iconic achievements, Cleese's influence extends far beyond the walls of the fictional hotel. His work with Monty Python, his solo projects, and his influence on modern comedy are all testaments to his enduring legacy.

John Cleese was a founding member of the legendary comedy troupe Monty Python, which revolutionized comedy with its absurd and surreal style. Monty Python's "Flying Circus" broke new ground in the late 1960s and 70s with its innovative sketches, non-linear narratives, and unique brand of humor. Cleese's memorable characters, such as the Minister of Silly Walks and the aggressive customer in the "Dead Parrot Sketch," became cultural icons. The group's influence can be seen in countless comedians and shows that followed, proving that Cleese and his cohorts were pioneers in redefining what comedy could be.

After Monty Python and "Fawlty Towers," Cleese continued to expand his comedic repertoire. He co-wrote and starred in the film "A Fish Called Wanda," which was a critical and commercial success, earning Cleese an Academy Award nomination for Best Original Screenplay. His role as the hapless lawyer Archie Leach showcased his ability to blend physical comedy with sophisticated humor. Cleese also became a sought-after voice actor, lending his distinctive voice to numerous animated films and television shows, further demonstrating his versatility.

In addition to his performances, John Cleese has been an influential writer and educator. He co-authored several books on comedy and creativity, including "So, Anyway...," an autobiography that offers insights into his life and career. Cleese has also given lectures and workshops on comedy writing and performance, sharing his extensive knowledge with aspiring comedians. His dedication to teaching and writing has helped to inspire a new generation of comedians and writers, ensuring that his impact on the comedy world will endure.

- **Early Beginnings**: John Cleese started his comedy career at Cambridge University, where he was a member of the Cambridge Footlights. His talent was quickly recognized, leading to opportunities in radio and television.

- **Monty Python's Success**: Cleese was instrumental in the success of Monty Python, contributing to iconic sketches like "The Ministry of Silly Walks" and "The Spanish Inquisition." The group's unique style set a new standard for sketch comedy.
- **The Origins of "Fawlty Towers"**: Cleese co-created "Fawlty Towers" with his then-wife Connie Booth, drawing inspiration from a real hotel owner they encountered in Torquay. The show's success cemented Cleese's status as a comedic genius.
- **Award-Winning Performance**: For his role in "A Fish Called Wanda," Cleese won a BAFTA for Best Actor in a Leading Role. The film's success highlighted his ability to craft and deliver sophisticated comedy.
- **Voice Acting**: Cleese has voiced characters in numerous animated films, including "Shrek 2" as King Harold and "The Jungle Book" as Kaa, showcasing his versatility and broad appeal.
- **James Bond Connection**: Cleese appeared in the James Bond films "The World Is Not Enough" and "Die Another Day" as Q's assistant, R. His presence added a touch of humor to the iconic spy series.
- **Educational Ventures**: Cleese co-founded Video Arts, a company that produced training films using humor to teach business skills. These films have been widely used in corporate training programs.
- **Autobiography**: His autobiography, "So, Anyway...," provides a humorous and insightful look into his life and career, offering fans a deeper understanding of his comedic philosophy and personal experiences.
- **Comedic Legacy**: Cleese's influence on comedy is evident in the work of numerous contemporary comedians who cite him as an inspiration. His approach to blending absurdity with sharp wit continues to resonate.

- **Continued Relevance**: Even in his later years, Cleese remains active in the entertainment industry, participating in new projects and tours. His enduring presence in comedy underscores his lasting impact and relevance.

Global Popularity and Adaptations of "Fawlty Towers"

"Fawlty Towers," despite its deeply British roots, has resonated with audiences worldwide, leading to numerous international adaptations. Each adaptation attempts to capture the essence of the original while infusing it with local flavor. However, the unique humor and dynamic of the original series often prove difficult to replicate. This is particularly evident in the adaptations made in Germany and Australia, where cultural differences and translation challenges led to some bizarre and fascinating results.

German Adaptation: "Zum Letzten Kliff"

In Germany, the show was adapted into "Zum Letzten Kliff" ("To the Last Cliff"), set in a fictional seaside hotel on the North Sea coast. The character of Basil Fawlty was renamed Fritz Wüst, and Sybil became Helga. Despite the attempt to stay true to the original's spirit, the German adaptation faced significant challenges:

Language Barriers and Humor: The translation of British humor into German posed a major challenge. Much of the original's wit and wordplay were lost in translation, and the subtlety of British sarcasm didn't always land with German audiences. As a result, the humor was often more straightforward and less nuanced.

Cultural Differences: German comedy typically emphasizes slapstick and situational humor over the dry wit and irony that "Fawlty Towers" is known for. To adapt, "Zum Letzten Kliff" incorporated more physical comedy and exaggerated situations, which sometimes came off as forced or unnatural compared to the original.

Mixed Reception: While the show did garner some interest, it never achieved the cult status of "Fawlty Towers." Critics noted that the charm and chemistry of the original cast were missing, and the adaptation struggled to find its footing in German popular culture.

" Uno, dos, tres"

Si, que, what"

I know nothing"

" Always you hit me!"

Australian Adaptation: "Fawlty Towers Down Under"

Australia also attempted to recreate the magic of "Fawlty Towers" with an adaptation set in a fictional outback hotel, humorously named "Fawlty Towers Down Under." The Australian version brought some uniquely bizarre elements to the table:

Crocodile Dundee Influence: The character equivalent to Basil Fawlty was a rugged, Crocodile Dundee-like figure named Bruce Fawlty. This portrayal starkly contrasted with John Cleese's neurotic and bumbling

Basil. Bruce's character was more physical and brash, catering to the Australian stereotype of rugged masculinity.

Outback Setting: The setting of the hotel in the outback introduced elements like wildlife and rugged terrain into the storyline. Episodes featured encounters with kangaroos, snakes, and even a runaway emu, adding a distinctly Australian flavour that was far removed from the quaint seaside town of Torquay.

Cultural Adaptation: The show tried to infuse Aussie humour, which is often characterised by a laid-back, self-deprecating style, into the episodes. This sometimes clashed with the original's fast-paced, high-energy comedy, leading to a disjointed feel.

Quirky Guest Characters: The adaptation introduced a variety of eccentric guest characters, including outback explorers, surfers, and indigenous Australian artists. While these characters added local colour, they sometimes felt out of place compared to the more universal guest archetypes in the original.

Reception and Legacy: "Fawlty Towers Down Under" had a short-lived run. While it was appreciated for its creativity and local touches, it couldn't match the original's charm and wit. The adaptation remains a curious footnote in the legacy of "Fawlty Towers," remembered more for its bold but ultimately unsuccessful attempt to localise a British classic.

Who Am I? - 20 Questions

Clues

1. I am a bumbling shopkeeper known for my tight-fisted ways and a stammer. I run a small grocery store and constantly harass my assistant.
   Who am I?

2. I am a lovable idiot who constantly gets into trouble with my brother Rodney. I'm always coming up with schemes to get rich quick.
   Who am I?

3. I am the inept hotel owner who is always rude to guests and staff alike. My wife, Sybil, often has to keep me in line.
   Who am I?

4. I am the clueless minister trying to navigate the complexities of British politics, often outwitted by my cunning civil servant.
   Who am I?

5. I am the lovable old cleaner in a department store, often seen daydreaming and causing mayhem in my workplace.
   Who am I?

6. I am the naive and cheerful office worker who adores my boss, David Brent. I have a peculiar laugh and a tendency to overshare.
   Who am I?

7. I am the stern, no-nonsense father in a working-class Manchester family, known for my catchphrase, "My arse!"
Who am I?

8. I am the bumbling vicar of Dibley, known for my love of chocolate and my quirky parishioners.
Who am I?

9. I am the neurotic, misanthropic radio DJ from Norwich, always desperate for another chance in the spotlight.
Who am I?

10. I am the laid-back shop assistant who dreams of a better life but is stuck working for my miserly uncle.
Who am I?

11. I am the uptight and often clueless boss of the Wernham Hogg paper company, always trying too hard to be liked by my employees.
Who am I?

12. I am the elderly, accident-prone member of the Home Guard in Walmington-on-Sea, known for my catchphrase, "Don't panic!"
Who am I?

13. I am the clueless yet lovable clerk in a department store, constantly making mistakes and causing chaos.
Who am I?

14. I am the overbearing matriarch of a family who runs a hotel on the English Riviera. My husband is often the butt of my jokes.
Who am I?

15. I am the naive but sweet-natured young man in a small London shop, often dreaming of a better life.
    Who am I?

16. I am the eccentric old man who lives with his family in a cluttered house and spends most of his time watching TV.
    Who am I?

17. I am the misanthropic, socially awkward office worker who constantly bickers with my best friend and roommate.
    Who am I?

18. I am the naive, well-intentioned priest assigned to a quirky parish on a remote island.
    Who am I?

19. I am the sly, cunning butler who secretly controls the household while serving my aristocratic employer.
    Who am I?

20. I am the stubborn and delusional leader of a ragtag group of old-fashioned home guardsmen during WWII.
    Who am I?

Answers

1. **Arkwright** from "Open All Hours"
2. **Del Boy Trotter** from "Only Fools and Horses"
3. **Basil Fawlty** from "Fawlty Towers"
4. **Jim Hacker** from "Yes Minister"
5. **Mrs. Slocombe** from "Are You Being Served?"
6. **Gareth Keenan** from "The Office (UK)"
7. **Jim Royle** from "The Royle Family"
8. **Geraldine Granger** from "The Vicar of Dibley"
9. **Alan Partridge** from "I'm Alan Partridge"
10. **Granville** from "Open All Hours"
11. **David Brent** from "The Office (UK)"
12. **Corporal Jones** from "Dad's Army"
13. **Frank Spencer** from "Some Mothers Do 'Ave 'Em"
14. **Sybil Fawlty** from "Fawlty Towers"
15. **Granville** from "Open All Hours"
16. **Albert Steptoe** from "Steptoe and Son"
17. **Mark Corrigan** from "Peep Show"
18. **Father Ted Crilly** from "Father Ted"
19. **Baldrick** from "Blackadder"
20. **Captain Mainwaring** from "Dad's Army"

Ricky Gervais

The Making of "The Office" and His Journey to Stardom

Ricky Gervais, born on June 25, 1961, in Reading, Berkshire, England, had a rather unassuming start. The youngest of four siblings, Ricky grew up in a working-class family. His father, a French-Canadian labourer, and his mother, a homemaker, instilled in him a love for laughter and storytelling. Young Ricky had a knack for making his family laugh, a skill that would later define his career. Despite his comedic flair, he initially pursued a degree in philosophy at University College London, where he also tried his hand at being a pop star with the new wave band Seona Dancing. The band didn't exactly set the world on fire, but it gave Ricky a taste of the limelight and a wealth of material for future comedic endeavours.

After a series of odd jobs and a stint as an assistant events manager at the University of London Union, Ricky Gervais found his way into radio in the most serendipitous way possible. He landed a job at Xfm, a London-based radio station, but not without a touch of his characteristic chaos. In need of an assistant, Ricky, who openly admitted to not knowing what he was doing, decided to hire the first person whose CV he pulled from the top of a pile. That person was Stephen Merchant, a towering figure with a sharp mind for comedy. This chance hiring proved to be pivotal in Ricky's career. The duo hit it off immediately, sharing a similar sense of humour and a creative vision that was destined to make waves. Their radio show became a cult favourite, filled with irreverent banter and hilarious segments that showcased Ricky's sharp wit and Stephen's deadpan delivery. It was during these radio sessions, filled with laughter and spontaneous comedy, that the seeds of "The Office" were planted, leading to one of the most iconic partnerships in modern comedy.

The Birth of "The Office"

"The Office" was born out of Ricky's and Stephen's shared experiences of dreary office environments and their desire to create something new in the comedy landscape. They wanted to capture the mundane absurdity of office life, with its petty politics and everyday frustrations. Ricky's portrayal of David Brent, the bumbling, self-deluded manager, was a masterstroke. Brent was the perfect blend of cringe and comedy, a character so painfully unaware of his own shortcomings that viewers couldn't help but laugh – and wince – at his antics. The show was a mockumentary, a format that was relatively fresh at the time, and it allowed for a raw, realistic portrayal of the characters and their interactions.

Breaking New Ground

"The Office" premiered on BBC Two in 2001 and quickly became a phenomenon. Its documentary-style format, coupled with its sharp writing and authentic performances, set it apart from traditional sitcoms. Ricky's Brent was a revelation – a character so deeply flawed yet oddly sympathetic that he became an instant icon. The show didn't shy away from awkward silences and uncomfortable moments, mining them for both humour and pathos. It wasn't just about the laughs; "The Office" was a poignant commentary on the human condition, capturing the desperation and hope that exists in every workplace.

The success of "The Office" didn't stop at the UK borders. It caught the attention of Hollywood, leading to an American adaptation produced by Greg Daniels. While the US version, starring Steve Carell as Michael Scott, eventually took on its own identity, it retained the spirit of the original. Ricky and Stephen were involved in the early stages, ensuring that the core elements were preserved. The American "Office" became a massive hit in its own right, running for nine seasons and solidifying the global legacy of the original series.

Beyond "The Office"

Following the success of "The Office," Ricky continued to push boundaries in comedy. He created and starred in "Extras," a series about the lives of background actors, which featured a host of celebrity cameos and showcased his knack for blending humour with heartfelt moments. Ricky's character, Andy Millman, was another triumph, capturing the desperation and absurdity of the entertainment industry. "Extras" earned critical acclaim and further cemented Ricky's status as a comedic genius.

Ricky's career also saw him return to his first love – stand-up comedy. Known for his biting wit and willingness to tackle controversial topics, his stand-up specials have been both celebrated and criticised. Ricky's humour often toes the line, but his fearlessness in addressing taboo subjects has garnered him a dedicated fan base. He's hosted the Golden Globes multiple times, each stint more notorious than the last, known for his scathing monologues that spare no one.

Ricky Gervais's impact on comedy is undeniable. From "The Office" to his stand-up specials, he has consistently pushed the envelope, challenging audiences and industry norms alike. His work has inspired a new generation of comedians to embrace authenticity and vulnerability in their craft. Beyond his professional achievements, Ricky is also known for his outspoken advocacy for animal rights and his philanthropic efforts. His journey from a working-class kid in Reading to an international comedy star is a testament to his talent, perseverance, and unwavering commitment to making people laugh – and think.

The Cringe-Worthy Brilliance of "The Office"

"The Office" is renowned for its masterful use of cringe comedy, a style that derives humour from socially awkward situations, uncomfortable interactions, and the characters' obliviousness to their own failings. Ricky Gervais, co-creator and star of the show, excelled in crafting these moments, making viewers squirm in their seats even as they laughed out loud.

David Brent's Cringe-Inducing Quotes and Moments

"There's no 'I' in the team. But there is a 'me' if you look hard enough."

David Brent, the bumbling manager of Wernham Hogg, often tries to appear wise and motivational but ends up exposing his self-centeredness and lack of insight. This quote exemplifies his misunderstanding of teamwork and leadership.

The Dance

- One of the most iconic moments in the series is David Brent's impromptu dance during a team-building exercise. Desperate to entertain and impress his staff, Brent performs an awkward, gyrating dance that leaves everyone in stunned silence. The scene perfectly encapsulates the character's delusional confidence and lack of self-awareness.

"If you're laughing, then I've already won."

Brent's frequent attempts to be the office comedian often backfire, as his jokes are either inappropriate or simply not funny. His desperate need for approval and validation through humour is painfully evident, creating a sense of second-hand embarrassment for the audience.

The Office Training Day

- In the episode "Training," David Brent hijacks a training seminar to perform his own rendition of "Freelove Freeway," a song he wrote. His earnest performance, coupled with the staff's visible discomfort and polite applause, makes for a quintessentially cringe-worthy scene.

The Blind Date

- In "The Office" Christmas special, David Brent goes on a series of blind dates. His awkward attempts at flirting and his inappropriate jokes make these scenes almost painful to watch. When he finally meets a woman who genuinely laughs at his jokes, the relief is palpable, but the journey there is a rollercoaster of cringe.

Gareth's Management Aspirations

- Gareth Keenan, played by Mackenzie Crook, is another source of awkward humour. His relentless desire to be taken seriously as a manager and his pedantic enforcement of office rules often lead to uncomfortable situations. For example, his interrogation of Tim about using the stapler without permission is both hilarious and excruciatingly awkward.

The Christmas Party

Tim's Confession

- The unrequited love story between Tim (Martin Freeman) and Dawn (Lucy Davis) reaches a cringe-inducing climax during the office Christmas party. Tim's heartfelt confession of his feelings to Dawn, only to be met with a polite but non-committal response, is a raw and painful moment that many viewers can relate to.

Why the Cringe Works?

The brilliance of "The Office" lies in its ability to mirror real-life awkwardness and social faux pas. The mockumentary format adds to the realism, making the characters' discomfort and flaws feel all the more genuine. The show doesn't just poke fun at these characters; it invites viewers to empathise with them, recognizing that everyone has moments of awkwardness and vulnerability.

Ricky Gervais and Stephen Merchant's writing captures the small, often unnoticed aspects of office life that can be both mundane and excruciating. The characters' desires for recognition, respect, and connection, juxtaposed with their frequent failures to achieve these goals, create a poignant and hilariously uncomfortable viewing experience.

30 Crazy and Bizarre Facts About "The Office"

1. **David Brent's Dance Was Improvised**: Ricky Gervais's infamous dance in "Charity" was not heavily rehearsed. He wanted it to feel spontaneous and cringeworthy, and it worked perfectly.
2. **Real Office Setting**: The set for Wernham Hogg was an actual office space in an industrial park, not a studio. This added to the authentic feel of the show.
3. **Stephen Merchant's Cameo**: Stephen Merchant, co-creator, made a cameo appearance as Oggy, the Oggmonster, in the episode "The Party." He was unrecognisable in his full-body costume.
4. **Gervais's Real Laughs**: Many of David Brent's laughs were real, as Gervais often cracked himself up during scenes, adding to the character's awkwardness.
5. **Short Seasons**: Unlike many TV shows, "The Office" UK had very short seasons—just six episodes each for its two main series, plus two Christmas specials.
6. **Multi-Talented Cast**: Mackenzie Crook, who played Gareth, is also a talented artist and illustrator. He created several pieces of art during filming breaks.

7. **Original Title**: The working title for "The Office" was "Paperweight." The change to "The Office" helped convey the show's mundane setting more effectively.
8. **Brent's Guitar Skills**: Ricky Gervais is actually an accomplished guitarist and wrote "Freelove Freeway," which Brent performs during the "Training" episode.
9. **Real Tears**: Lucy Davis, who played Dawn, actually cried during her character's emotional scenes, such as Tim's confession at the Christmas party. The tears were genuine, adding to the authenticity of the moment.
10. **Ricky's US Office Cameo**: Ricky Gervais's David Brent made a memorable cameo in the American version of "The Office," where he meets Steve Carell's Michael Scott in a hilarious encounter.
11. **Casting Coincidence**: Martin Freeman, who played Tim, and Mackenzie Crook (Gareth) later starred together in "The Hobbit" trilogy, though their characters in "The Office" were starkly different.
12. **Real-Life Office Dynamics**: Ricky Gervais and Stephen Merchant based many characters on people they knew from their own office experiences, adding layers of realism to the interactions.
13. **Fan Theories**: There are numerous fan theories about the show, including one that posits that David Brent is an older, failed version of Tim Canterbury, due to their similar traits and mannerisms.
14. **Instant Classic**: The pilot episode was not an instant success. It was only after a rerun and word-of-mouth that the show gained a significant following.
15. **Authentic Reactions**: Often, scenes were shot without rehearsals to capture the cast's authentic reactions, making the awkward moments even more genuine.
16. **Gervais's Marketing Background**: Ricky Gervais worked in marketing before his comedy career took off, which

informed his portrayal of the corporate world in "The Office."

17. **International Versions**: Aside from the well-known American adaptation, "The Office" has been adapted in several other countries, including India, France, and Israel.
18. **Real Paper Company**: Wernham Hogg was named after actual companies—Wernham, a demolition firm, and Hogg Robinson, a travel company.
19. **Gervais's Brent on Tour**: Ricky Gervais took David Brent on tour after the show, performing music and comedy in character, further blurring the lines between fiction and reality.
20. **Office Artwork**: The art in the office was created by local artists to reflect the uninspired corporate environment, adding another layer of realism to the set.
21. **Unexpected Popularity**: The series found unexpected popularity in Sweden, where the dry British humour resonated deeply with the Swedish audience.
22. **Budget Constraints**: The show had a modest budget, leading to creative solutions for filming and set design that contributed to its realistic look.
23. **First Sitcom Mockumentary**: "The Office" is credited with popularising the mockumentary format in sitcoms, influencing shows like "Parks and Recreation" and "Modern Family."
24. **Hidden Easter Eggs**: The series contains numerous hidden Easter eggs, such as subtle references to Ricky Gervais's previous work and inside jokes between the creators.
25. **Christmas Special Success**: The Christmas specials drew record-breaking viewership numbers in the UK, cementing the show's legacy.
26. **Gervais's Directing Style**: Ricky Gervais often directed scenes to be more improvisational, allowing actors to bring their own spin to the dialogue and actions.

27. **Merchant's Inspiration**: Stephen Merchant was inspired by his time working as a temp in an office, bringing personal experiences to the script.
28. **Merchandise**: The success of "The Office" led to various merchandise, including David Brent action figures and office-themed board games.
29. **Post-Office Careers**: Many cast members went on to have successful careers in film and television, with Martin Freeman starring in "Sherlock" and "The Hobbit" and Mackenzie Crook creating and starring in "Detectorists."
30. **Ricky's Cameos**: Gervais's character, David Brent, made surprise appearances in various formats, including YouTube videos and charity specials, keeping the character alive beyond the series.

No Rehearsals, Just Raw Comedy

What makes the dance scene particularly fascinating is that it was almost entirely improvised. Gervais decided not to rehearse the dance beforehand to ensure that the performance would feel as spontaneous and awkward as possible. The cast and crew were not given any details about what the dance would entail, which allowed for genuine reactions of shock and amusement. This approach added an extra layer of authenticity to the scene, capturing the true essence of Brent's character and the uncomfortable hilarity that ensued.

Crew's Reaction and Retakes

The crew struggled to keep straight faces during the filming of the dance scene. There were multiple takes, not because Gervais made mistakes, but because the cast and crew couldn't stop laughing. Gervais himself had to stifle his laughter at times, staying in character as the oblivious Brent. This behind-the-scenes camaraderie and the genuine amusement of those involved contributed to the scene's success. It was a perfect example of how "The Office" leveraged real, human reactions to create moments of comedy that felt true to life.

Life on the Road: The Movie Spin-Off and Ricky Gervais's Musical Past

In 2016, Ricky Gervais brought back his iconic character, David Brent, for a movie spin-off titled "David Brent: Life on the Road." The film follows Brent, now a travelling salesman, as he pursues his dream of becoming a rock star. This return to the character allowed Gervais to explore new comedic territory while staying true to the awkward, cringe-inducing humour that made "The Office" so beloved. The movie captures Brent's delusional ambition and desperate need for validation, delivering a blend of comedy and pathos.

"Life on the Road" sees David Brent financing his own tour with his band, Foregone Conclusion, using his pension and making numerous sacrifices. The film portrays Brent's unwavering belief in his musical talent, despite clear evidence to the contrary. His interactions with his bandmates, who are clearly there for the money, and his futile attempts to impress his colleagues, form the core of the movie's humour. The film's mockumentary style stays true to "The Office," giving it a familiar feel while delving deeper into Brent's personal aspirations and insecurities.

Ricky's Musical Past: Seona Dancing

Ricky Gervais's portrayal of Brent's musical endeavours in "Life on the Road" is informed by his own real-life experiences as a musician. In the early 1980s, before he became a household name in comedy, Gervais was part of a new wave band called Seona Dancing. The band consisted of Gervais as the lead vocalist and his friend Bill Macrae on keyboards. Their music was heavily influenced by the synth-pop sounds of the era, reminiscent of bands like Duran Duran and Spandau Ballet.

Seona Dancing signed with London Records and released two singles, "More to Lose" and "Bitter Heart," in 1983. Despite their efforts, the singles failed to make a significant impact on the UK charts. However, "More to Lose" became an unexpected hit in the Philippines, where it achieved cult status and was extensively played on the radio. The band eventually disbanded, but Gervais's brief stint as a pop star provided him with a wealth of material for his later comedic work.

Gervais's experience with Seona Dancing is reflected in many of his comedic projects, most notably in David Brent's character. Brent's cringeworthy songs and misguided belief in his own talent are exaggerated versions of Gervais's real-life experiences in the music industry. In "Life on the Road," songs like "Lady Gypsy" and "Equality Street" showcase Brent's earnest yet hilariously out-of-touch approach to songwriting, blending genuine musical talent with comedic absurdity.

"David Brent: Life on the Road" received mixed reviews from critics but was appreciated by fans of "The Office" for its nostalgic value and Gervais's committed performance. The film serves as a fitting continuation of Brent's story, exploring themes of ambition, delusion, and the human desire for acceptance. While it may not have reached the same heights as "The Office," the movie solidified David Brent's place in the pantheon of iconic comedy characters.

As you reach the halfway mark of *The Ultimate British Sitcom Challenge*, we hope you're enjoying the nostalgic trip through these classic comedies. But the fun doesn't stop here! Scan the QR code for free content and keep the laughs coming as you dive deeper into the world of British sitcoms.

Dad's Army

Dad's Army Quiz: 20 Questions

1. What is the name of the town where "Dad's Army" is set?

    A. Walmington-on-Sea
    B. Eastbourne
    C. Basingstoke
    D. Clacton-on-Sea

2. Who is the captain of the Home Guard platoon in "Dad's Army"?

    A. Sergeant Wilson
    B. Corporal Jones
    C. Captain Mainwaring
    D. Private Pike

3. What is Corporal Jones's famous catchphrase?

    A. "Don't panic!"
    B. "You stupid boy!"
    C. "Permission to speak, sir!"
    D. "We're doomed!"

4. What role does Private Pikes mother, Mavis Pike, play in the series?

    A. The platoon's secretary
    B. The town's postmistress
    C. The platoon's cook
    D. She runs the local tea shop

5. Who often says "We're doomed!"?

    A. Private Walker

    B. Private Frazer
    C. Private Godfrey
    D. Captain Mainwaring

6. What is the name of the bank where Captain Mainwaring works?

    A. Walmington Bank
    B. Mainwaring & Co.
    C. Walmington-on-Sea Bank
    D. Swallow Bank

7. Who is the town's verger and a constant source of trouble for the platoon?

    A. Mr. Yeatman
    B. Mr. Hodges
    C. Mr. Gordon
    D. Mr. Wilson

8. What does Private Frazer do for a living?

    A. Butcher
    B. Undertaker
    C. Fishmonger
    D. Farmer

9. Which character is known for wearing a scarf?

    A. Private Pike
    B. Private Frazer
    C. Sergeant Wilson
    D. Private Walker

10. What is Sergeant Wilson's first name?

    A. Arthur
    B. John
    C. Charles
    D. James

11. Who plays Captain Mainwaring in the series?

    A. John Le Mesurier
    B. Arnold Ridley
    C. Arthur Lowe
    D. Clive Dunn

12. What is the platoon's primary mission?

    A. Defending against German spies
    B. Guarding the coast
    C. Training new recruits
    D. Civil defence during air raids

13. Which character often reminisces about his service in Sudan?

    A. Captain Mainwaring
    B. Private Walker
    C. Corporal Jones
    D. Private Godfrey

14. Who is known for his catchphrase "You stupid boy!"?

    A. Captain Mainwaring
    B. Sergeant Wilson
    C. Private Pike
    D. Corporal Jones

15. What is the name of Private Godfrey's sister?

    A. Dolly
    B. Cissy
    C. Mabel
    D. Edith

16. Which character is an elderly butcher who fought in the Boer War?

    A. Private Walker
    B. Private Frazer
    C. Corporal Jones
    D. Private Godfrey

17. **What is the title of the theme song for "Dad's Army"?**

   A. "Who Do You Think You Are Kidding, Mr. Hitler?"
   B. "Keep the Home Fires Burning"
   C. "We'll Meet Again"
   D. "Bless 'Em All"

18. **Who often provides black market goods to the platoon?**

   A. Private Pike
   B. Private Walker
   C. Sergeant Wilson
   D. Private Godfrey

19. **Which character has a mysterious, upper-class background?**

   A. Private Frazer
   B. Captain Mainwaring
   C. Sergeant Wilson
   D. Private Walker

20. **In which decade did "Dad's Army" originally air?**

   A. 1950s
   B. 1960s
   C. 1970s
   D. 1980s

Answers

1. What is the name of the town where "Dad's Army" is set?

- **Walmington-on-Sea** - Walmington-on-Sea is a fictional seaside town created for the series, set on the south coast of England during World War II.

2. Who is the captain of the Home Guard platoon in "Dad's Army"?

- **C. Captain Mainwaring** - Captain George Mainwaring, played by Arthur Lowe, is the pompous and determined leader of the Walmington-on-Sea Home Guard.

3. What is Corporal Jones's famous catchphrase?

- **"Don't panic!"** - Corporal Jack Jones, portrayed by Clive Dunn, frequently shouts "Don't panic!" in moments of crisis, often causing more panic among the platoon.

4. What role does Private Pikes mother, Mavis Pike, play in the series?

- **She runs the local tea shop** - Mavis Pike, played by Janet Davies, is a protective mother who runs a tea shop and is very concerned about her son, Frank Pike.

5. Who often says "We're doomed!"?

- **B. Private Frazer** - Private James Frazer, a Scottish undertaker played by John Laurie, is known for his pessimistic outlook and his catchphrase, "We're doomed!"

6. What is the name of the bank where Captain Mainwaring works?

- **Swallow Bank** - Captain Mainwaring is the manager of Swallow Bank, which serves as a central location for many of the series' scenes.

7. Who is the town's verger and a constant source of trouble for the platoon?

- **B. Mr. Hodges** - Mr. Maurice Yeatman, the verger, often causes trouble, but it's ARP Warden William Hodges, played by Bill Pertwee, who is the platoon's main antagonist.

8. What does Private Frazer do for a living?

- **C. Fishmonger** - Private Frazer is a dour Scottish fishmonger with a side job as an undertaker.

9. Which character is known for wearing a scarf?

- **Private Pike** - Private Frank Pike, played by Ian Lavender, is often seen wearing a scarf, reflecting his mother's overprotective nature.

10. **What is Sergeant Wilson's first name?**

    - **Arthur** - Sergeant Arthur Wilson, portrayed by John Le Mesurier, is Captain Mainwaring's suave and laid-back second-in-command.

11. **Who plays Captain Mainwaring in the series?**

    - **C. Arthur Lowe** - Arthur Lowe's portrayal of Captain Mainwaring is considered one of the most iconic performances in British television comedy.

12. **What is the platoon's primary mission?**

    - **B. Guarding the coast** - The Home Guard platoon's main duty is to defend the British coastline against potential German invasion during World War II.

13. **Which character often reminisces about his service in Sudan?**

    - **C. Corporal Jones** - Corporal Jones frequently shares exaggerated and humorous stories of his time serving in the Sudan campaign under General Kitchener.

14. **Who is known for his catchphrase "You stupid boy!"?**

    - **Captain Mainwaring** - Captain Mainwaring often directs this phrase at Private Pike, highlighting Pike's youthful naivety.

15. **What is the name of Private Godfrey's sister?**

    - **B. Cissy** - Cissy Godfrey is Private Charles Godfrey's sister, and they live together in their quaint cottage.

16. **Which character is an elderly butcher who fought in the Boer War?**

    - **C. Corporal Jones** - Corporal Jones's military experience dates back to the Boer War, making him one of the oldest members of the platoon.

17. **What is the title of the theme song for "Dad's Army"?**
    - **"Who Do You Think You Are Kidding, Mr. Hitler?"** - The theme song, written by Jimmy Perry and Derek Taverner and sung by Bud Flanagan, sets the tone for the show's comedic take on wartime Britain.

18. **Who often provides black market goods to the platoon?**
    - **B. Private Walker** - Private Joe Walker, played by James Beck, is the platoon's spiv who deals in black market goods and can procure almost anything for a price.

19. **Which character has a mysterious, upper-class background?**
    - **C. Sergeant Wilson** - Sergeant Wilson's upper-class background is hinted at throughout the series, and he is often seen as more refined and cultured than his comrades.

20. **In which decade did "Dad's Army" originally air?**
    - **B. 1960s** - "Dad's Army" first aired in 1968 and continued until 1977, becoming one of the most beloved British sitcoms of all time.

The 20 Best "Dad's Army" Moments

20. A Stain on His Character (Turkey Dinner, December 1974)
- At a festive dinner for the town's OAPs, Pike accidentally tips gravy down Captain Mainwaring's best dinner jacket. This perfectly captures the series' blend of slapstick humour and the rigid, pompous nature of Mainwaring's character.

19. The Green-Eyed Monster (The Honourable Man, November 1973)
- Mainwaring is furious to learn that Wilson has been granted a title, exacerbated by Pike and his mother's reactions. Mainwaring's jealousy and the ensuing hilarity underline the class tensions within the platoon.

18. The Special Relationship (My British Buddy, November 1973)

- Mainwaring is told a visiting US colonel will greet him with, "Howdy partner, put it there." His confusion and stiff-upper-lip response highlight the cultural differences in a humorous way.

17. We're All Wet, Mr. Mainwaring! (The Royal Train, November 1973)

- The platoon stands at attention to salute the King's train, oblivious to the fact that they are standing next to a water trough, leading to a soaking. This scene epitomises the comedic misfortune that befalls the Home Guard.

16. The Day the Balloon Went Pop (Battle of the Giants!, December 1971)

- During a training exercise, Mainwaring's shot accidentally hits a distant balloon. Wilson's understated "Good heavens!" and Mainwaring's incredulous reaction, "What do you mean, 'Good heavens'?" is classic British humour.

15. Warden in the Water (Battle of the Giants!, December 1971)

- A typically belligerent ARP Warden Hodges gets pushed by Wilson off a bridge into the river below, showcasing the ongoing rivalry and physical comedy that fans love.

14. "Ask Your Friends to Have Some Tea" (The Battle of Godfrey's Cottage, March 1969)

- The Home Guard commandeers Godfrey's home, while his sisters carry on as if nothing unusual is happening, even as bullets start to fly. The absurdity and the stiff-upper-lip attitude of the sisters make this moment unforgettable.

13. Herd the One About the Pantomime Cow? (Operation Kilt, March 1969)

- Frazer and Walker, disguised as a pantomime cow, try to pass through a field of cows, only to be confronted by a bull. The slapstick humour and ridiculous situations are hallmarks of the show's charm.

12. Pipe Down, Frazer! (If the Cap Fits…, November 1972)

- Frazer delights at Mainwaring's imminent humiliation at a regimental dinner where he's just been asked to play the bagpipes, only to be flabbergasted by Mainwaring's secret piping skills.

11. Hair Today (Keep Young and Beautiful, October 1972)

- Wilson laughs at Mainwaring's toupee, only to be met with the retort, "Watch it, Wilson, you might snap your girdle!" This exchange perfectly encapsulates their comedic dynamic.

10. Jones Goes for a Spin (Don't Forget the Diver, October 1970)

- Attempting to capture a windmill being defended by the rival Eastgate platoon, the overenthusiastic Jones gets caught in the sails, then plummets into the river. The physical comedy is executed brilliantly.

9. "Stupid Boy" (When You've Got to Go, September 1975)

- At a supper to give him a call-up send-off, Pike finally admits that due to his rare blood type, he won't be joining the RAF. Mainwaring's exasperated "Stupid boy" has become an enduring catchphrase.

8. Old Po-Face is My Brother (My Brother and I, December 1975)

- Alcoholic novelty salesman Barry Mainwaring introduces himself to an incredulous and gleeful Frazer, adding a layer of complexity and humour to Mainwaring's background.

7. Mystery Woman Revealed (Getting the Bird, October 1972)

- Frazer accidentally learns that Wilson has a grown-up daughter and swears surprisingly heartfelt discretion, adding depth to the usually prickly character.

6. "To the Home Guard" (Never Too Old, November 1977)

- In the final episode, Mainwaring gives the men a pep talk, ending with Wilson suggesting a special toast. This poignant moment reflects the camaraderie built over the series.

5. A Brief Encounter for the Captain (Mum's Army, November 1970)

- Mainwaring becomes romantically involved with Mrs. Gray, a volunteer in the women's section. Their relationship and her departure reveal a softer, more vulnerable side of Mainwaring.

4. The Old Empty Barn (Gorilla Warfare, November 1974)

- Out on a field exercise, the men bed down in a barn and brace themselves for one of Frazer's ghost stories. His tale, "the old empty barn... there was nothing in it!" is a masterclass in anticlimactic humour.

3. Cardinal Puff-Puff (Fallen Idol, December 1970)

- At a weekend training camp, Mainwaring struggles with a tortuously complicated officers' drinking game, leading to hilarious confusion and whisky-soaked chaos.

2. Hidden Hero (Branded, November 1969)

- Shunned after revealing he was a conscientious objector during WWI, modest Godfrey saves Mainwaring's life from a smoke-filled hut. The platoon learns he was awarded the Military Medal for bravery, a deeply moving moment.

1. "Don't Tell Him, Pike!" (The Deadly Attachment, October 1973)

- In this legendary scene, Mainwaring instructs Pike not to reveal his name to a German U-boat captain. Mainwaring's command, "Don't tell him, Pike!" immediately after Pike's name is asked, is an unforgettable piece of comedic timing that has been voted the funniest line in British TV history.

The Secret History of 'Comedy's Finest Half-Hour'

To delve into the history of "Dad's Army," one must navigate through a near-military environment. Security measures like speed bumps, vehicle checks, and CCTV are all present on the grounds of BBC Monitoring in Caversham, Berkshire, where the paperwork about the show's creation is meticulously stored. These stringent protections are due to the sensitive nature of the archives, which also support the intelligence services. It's fitting that the records of "Dad's Army," the BBC's most enduringly valuable program, are kept under such watchful eyes.

"Dad's Army" premiered on July 31, 1968, and despite the show ending in 1977, its reruns continue to top BBC Two ratings. The journey began with producer-director David Croft and co-writer Jimmy Perry, who each received £200 for a script originally titled "The Fighting Tigers." The script was based on Perry's WWII experiences with the Local Defence Volunteers, later known as the Home Guard. Interestingly, Arthur Lowe, who portrayed the pompous Captain Mainwaring, was paid £170 and two shillings for his role.

The series wasn't initially embraced with open arms. Arthur Lowe, who played Captain Mainwaring, often disparaged the script. He would hide it behind radiators or leave it with his driver, not wanting to bring it into his home. During the filming of the first series, John Le Mesurier, who played Sergeant Wilson, reportedly told colleagues at the BBC bar that the show would be a complete disaster. These behind-the-scenes tensions were compounded by concerns at the BBC about offending war veterans and their families.

The Budget and Star Power

The budget for the first series reflects an interesting hierarchy: John Le Mesurier was paid £209, nine shillings, and sixpence, as he was initially regarded as the star. Arthur Lowe, meanwhile, earned £170 and two shillings. Michael Grade, then a junior showbiz agent, negotiated third billing and equal pay for Clive Dunn, who played Lance Corporal Jones. Dunn, though only 47, convincingly portrayed the much older Jones.

Despite initial reservations from the BBC, "Dad's Army" quickly became a hit. One viewer even offered to loan the production team his "overcoat and battle dress outfit." Letters from fans began pouring in, with suggestions and compliments that highlighted the show's wide appeal. By the third episode, critics began to recognize its quality. Barry Took, a distinguished comedy writer, even wrote to David Croft, praising the show's scripts, casting, and direction.

The famous "Don't tell him, Pike!" The scene from "The Deadly Attachment" is a prime example of the show's brilliance. Ian Lavender, who played Pike, struggled to keep a straight face during the filming. Arthur Lowe, aware of the significance of the punchline, felt the pressure, leading to a slight flub before delivering the iconic line. Despite the tension, the scene came together perfectly, becoming one of the most memorable moments in British television history.

As "Dad's Army" celebrates its 50th anniversary, its legacy remains strong. Ian Lavender, the only surviving member of the main cast, reflects on the show's universal appeal. He believes that the show's enduring popularity stems from its ability to entertain audiences of all ages. Despite the niche-driven nature of modern TV, "Dad's Army" continues to be a beloved family favourite.

Initially, the BBC was nervous about the show's potential to offend those who had served in the war. This led to the removal of footage of Nazi troops and displaced refugees from the opening titles. However, the show quickly won over its target audience. A Home Guard veteran named Private Huntley wrote to congratulate the makers, and many others sent in anecdotes and suggestions, further cementing the show's success.

Despite early scepticism, the cast grew to appreciate their roles. Ian Lavender, who played Pike, fondly recalls the knitted scarf his character's mother gave him. Contrary to the grumbling of some colleagues, Lavender expresses immense pride in being part of the show. He appreciates the gentle humour and enduring charm of "Dad's Army," finding it a pleasant reminder of a more innocent time.

"Dad's Army" has earned its place as a classic, thanks to the dedicated cast and crew who brought the series to life. Its blend of humour, nostalgia, and character-driven comedy continues to captivate audiences, proving that good storytelling stands the test of time.

Yes Minister

A Hilarious Insight into Inside Politics

"Yes Minister" is a classic British sitcom that aired from 1980 to 1984, offering viewers a satirical glimpse into the complexities and absurdities of government bureaucracy. The show centres on the political career of Jim Hacker, a newly appointed minister, and his interactions with his Permanent Secretary, Sir Humphrey Appleby. Through its clever writing and sharp wit, "Yes Minister" provided audiences with a unique understanding of the often opaque world of politics.

At the heart of "Yes Minister" are its brilliantly crafted characters. Jim Hacker, played by Paul Eddington, is the well-meaning but often clueless Minister of Administrative Affairs. Sir Humphrey Appleby, portrayed by Nigel Hawthorne, is the cunning and manipulative civil servant who knows the ins and outs of the government machinery better than anyone. Bernard Woolley, played by Derek Fowlds, is the Principal Private Secretary caught between the two. Their interactions and power struggles reveal much about the dynamics of political life.

One of the show's central themes is the manipulation and manoeuvring that occurs behind the scenes in politics. Sir Humphrey is a master of this art, using his vast knowledge and experience to outwit Hacker at every turn. His ability to spin information, bury inconvenient facts, and present half-truths as gospel is both impressive and terrifying. Through Sir Humphrey's antics, viewers gain an understanding of how information can be controlled and how bureaucratic inertia can be used to maintain the status quo.

"Yes Minister" brilliantly showcases the concept of bureaucratic inertia – the idea that government systems and structures are resistant to change. Sir Humphrey often employs red tape and convoluted procedures to delay or derail Hacker's initiatives. This not only highlights the difficulty of implementing reforms but also satirises the inefficiencies inherent in large bureaucratic organisations. The show's portrayal of endless committee meetings, reports, and consultations is both hilarious and painfully accurate.

Throughout the series, Jim Hacker is acutely aware of public opinion and the media's influence on his political career. Episodes frequently depict his efforts to manage public perception, often leading to comedic situations where he must backtrack or spin his previous statements. This aspect of the show highlights the precarious balance politicians must maintain between their public persona and their behind-the-scenes actions, emphasising the performative nature of modern politics.

The Civil Service vs. Politicians

A recurring theme in "Yes Minister" is the tension between elected officials and the civil service. While politicians like Jim Hacker are focused on short-term gains and re-election, civil servants like Sir Humphrey are depicted as being more concerned with preserving the continuity and stability of the government. This dynamic creates a constant push and pull, with Sir Humphrey often thwarting Hacker's more radical proposals in favour of maintaining the status quo.

Despite its comedic approach, "Yes Minister" is grounded in a keen understanding of political realities. Many of the scenarios depicted in the show, from budgetary constraints to interdepartmental rivalries, are based on real issues faced by governments. The show's writers, Antony Jay and Jonathan Lynn, conducted extensive research and consulted with political insiders to ensure authenticity. This blend of satire and realism helps viewers appreciate the complexities and challenges of governing.

The dialogue in "Yes Minister" is peppered with memorable quotes and catchphrases that have become part of popular culture. Sir Humphrey's verbose explanations and obfuscations are particularly iconic. Phrases like "In the fullness of time" and "I foresee all sorts of unforeseen problems" capture the essence of bureaucratic double-speak. These lines not only entertain but also provide insight into the ways language can be used to confuse and control.

While "Yes Minister" focuses on the political and bureaucratic machinations, it also humanises its characters. Jim Hacker's earnestness, Sir Humphrey's loyalty to the civil service, and Bernard's moral dilemmas add depth to their portrayals. The show balances its satire with moments of genuine humanity, reminding viewers that behind every political decision are individuals with their own motivations and struggles.

"Yes Minister" has left a lasting legacy in the world of political satire. Its influence can be seen in later shows like "The Thick of It" and "Veep," which also explore the absurdities of political life. By combining sharp wit with insightful commentary, "Yes Minister" has educated and entertained generations of viewers. It remains a touchstone for understanding the intricate dance between politics and bureaucracy, proving that sometimes, laughter is the best way to illuminate the truth.

The Thick of It: The Next Evolution in Political Satire

Following in the footsteps of "Yes Minister," "The Thick of It" premiered in 2005, bringing a new, modern twist to political satire. Created by Armando Iannucci, the show takes place in the fictional Department of Social Affairs and Citizenship and offers a blisteringly sharp, profanity-laden take on the workings of government. It maintains the essence of "Yes Minister" by showcasing the absurdities and inefficiencies of political life but updates it with a contemporary edge and a more cynical tone.

At the center of "The Thick of It" is Malcolm Tucker, played by Peter Capaldi. Tucker is the aggressive, foul-mouthed Director of Communications for the government, whose main job is to keep the

Prime Minister and his cabinet members out of trouble. His role is similar to Sir Humphrey Appleby's in that he manipulates situations behind the scenes, but his methods are far more ruthless and explicit. The show's ministers and civil servants are constantly navigating the treacherous waters of public opinion, media scrutiny, and internal power struggles.

"The Thick of It" takes political manipulation to new heights. Malcolm Tucker's ability to twist and turn every situation to his advantage, often through sheer intimidation and verbal barrages, provides a starkly humorous yet sobering look at the dark arts of spin. One of Tucker's iconic lines, "I'll tell you who you are, you're a fucking nobody! That's who you are!" epitomizes his brutal approach to crisis management.

Like "Yes Minister," "The Thick of It" is deeply rooted in reality. The show's creators consulted with real politicians, advisors, and journalists to ensure authenticity. The result is a series that feels uncannily true to life, reflecting the chaotic, often farcical nature of modern governance. The show's use of handheld cameras and improvised dialogue adds to its documentary-like feel, making the satire even more biting.

"The Thick of It" is packed with memorable quotes and hilarious gags that have become part of British pop culture. Here are a few standout lines:

- **Malcolm Tucker:** "Climb the mountain of conflict? You fucking bet I'm going to climb it. I'll climb it in my shorts. I'll climb it while carrying a fucking sandbag!"
- **Malcolm Tucker:** "He's as useless as a marzipan dildo."
- **Glenn Cullen:** "The only reason the PM would want this is if he wants to say a fucking flat 'no' to it. This is one of those political things where you think you understand it, then you don't, then you think you do again but you don't, but at the end, you realize you never understood it, but that's when you finally understand it."

- **Ollie Reeder:** "You can't just lock people in a cupboard. This isn't Spain."

"The Thick of It" has had a profound influence on how political satire is approached. It paved the way for other shows like "Veep," another Iannucci creation, which brings the same biting humor to the American political scene. The success of "The Thick of It" lies in its ability to blend humor with a sharp critique of political processes, much like "Yes Minister," but with a rawer, more confrontational style.

Where "Yes Minister" highlighted the subtle, almost genteel manipulations of a past era, "The Thick of It" dives headfirst into the chaos and media frenzy of modern politics. It portrays a world where public perception is constantly managed, scandals are daily occurrences, and the line between competence and ineptitude is razor-thin. This reflects a more jaded view of politics, resonating with audiences who are increasingly skeptical of their leaders.

Despite its harsh satire, "The Thick of It" also humanizes its characters. Malcolm Tucker, while ruthless, is shown to be under immense pressure and even vulnerable at times. The ministers and their aides, despite their often comical incompetence, are depicted as people trying to navigate an impossible system. This balance of harsh critique and character depth adds layers to the comedy, making it both entertaining and thought-provoking.

"The Thick of It" stands as a worthy successor to "Yes Minister," taking political satire to new heights with its modern approach. Its blend of sharp writing, memorable characters, and realistic portrayal of government makes it a cornerstone of contemporary comedy. By exposing the absurdities of political life with both humor and insight, "The Thick of It" continues the legacy of educating and entertaining audiences, proving that the world of politics is as ripe for satire today as it was decades ago.

The Black Adder Quiz

Questions

1. Who played the character of Edmund Blackadder in "The Black Adder" series?

    A. Hugh Laurie
    B. Stephen Fry
    C. Rowan Atkinson
    D. Tony Robinson

2. What is the title of the first episode of "The Black Adder"?

    A. "The Foretelling"
    B. "Born to Be King"
    C. "The Archbishop"
    D. "The Queen of Spain's Beard"

3. Who is the bumbling servant of Edmund Blackadder throughout the series?

    A. Baldrick
    B. Percy
    C. George
    D. Melchett

4. In "Blackadder II," which Queen does Edmund serve?

    A. Queen Victoria
    B. Queen Elizabeth I
    C. Queen Mary
    D. Queen Anne

5. What is Baldrick's first name?

    A. William

B. Harry
C. S. Baldrick
D. He does not have a first name

6. Which war is depicted in "Blackadder Goes Forth"?

A. The Napoleonic Wars
B. The Crimean War
C. The First World War
D. The Second World War

7. In "Blackadder the Third," who is Prince Regent?

A. Prince George
B. Prince Charles
C. Prince Edward
D. Prince Harry

8. What profession does Edmund Blackadder take on in "Blackadder the Third"?

A. A butler
B. A general
C. A sailor
D. A scientist

9. Who played the role of Queen Elizabeth I in "Blackadder II"?

A. Miranda Richardson
B. Helen Mirren
C. Emma Thompson
D. Judi Dench

10. What is the main plot of the final episode of "Blackadder Goes Forth"?

A. A court-martial trial
B. A Christmas truce
C. The Battle of the Somme
D. An escape attempt from the trenches

11. What is the name of Blackadder's foolish friend in "Blackadder II"?

    A. Percy
    B. George
    C. Hugh
    D. Darling

12. Who wrote "The Black Adder" series alongside Rowan Atkinson?

    A. Ben Elton
    B. Richard Curtis
    C. Stephen Fry
    D. John Cleese

13. In "Blackadder's Christmas Carol," what role does Edmund play?

    A. A generous man who becomes mean
    B. A mean man who becomes generous
    C. A soldier during Christmas
    D. A servant at a Christmas feast

14. What is the name of the episode where Blackadder tries to become Archbishop of Canterbury?

    A. "Money"
    B. "Beer"
    C. "The Archbishop"
    D. "The Witchsmeller Pursuivant"

15. In "Blackadder II," what is the title of the episode where Blackadder must marry Princess Leia of Hungary?

    A. "Bells"
    B. "Potato"
    C. "Head"
    D. "Chains"

16. Who played the role of Captain Darling in "Blackadder Goes Forth"?

    A. Hugh Laurie
    B. Tim McInnerny
    C. Stephen Fry
    D. Tony Robinson

17. What is the main theme of the episode "Beer" in "Blackadder II"?

    A. A duel with a rival
    B. Hosting a drinking contest
    C. A witch trial
    D. A love affair

18. What historical period does "Blackadder the Third" take place in?

    A. The Tudor period
    B. The Georgian era
    C. The Victorian era
    D. The Edwardian era

19. What is the ultimate fate of the characters in "Blackadder Goes Forth"?

    A. They escape to safety
    B. They die in battle
    C. They are captured by the enemy
    D. They survive and return home

20. In "Blackadder II," what is Blackadder's relationship with Lord Melchett?

    A. They are best friends
    B. They are rivals
    C. Melchett is Blackadder's servant
    D. Blackadder is Melchett's mentor

Answers - The Black Adder Quiz

1. **Who played the character of Edmund Blackadder in "The Black Adder" series?**

   - **C. Rowan Atkinson** - Rowan Atkinson brought Edmund Blackadder to life with his sharp wit and distinctive performance, making the character iconic in British comedy.

2. **What is the title of the first episode of "The Black Adder"?**

   - **"The Foretelling"** - "The Foretelling" sets the stage for the series, introducing the historical setting and the lineage of the Blackadder family.

3. **Who is the bumbling servant of Edmund Blackadder throughout the series?**

   - **Baldrick** - Played by Tony Robinson, Baldrick is known for his "cunning plans," which are usually absurd and impractical.

4. **In "Blackadder II," which Queen does Edmund serve?**

   - **B. Queen Elizabeth I** - Queen Elizabeth I, portrayed by Miranda Richardson, is a whimsical and often capricious ruler, providing much of the series' humor.

5. **What is Baldrick's first name?**

   - **He does not have a first name** - Baldrick's first name is never revealed, adding to the character's mysterious and comical nature.

6. **Which war is depicted in "Blackadder Goes Forth"?**

   - **C. The First World War** - The series is set in the trenches of WWI, offering a darkly humorous take on the horrors of war.

7. In "Blackadder the Third," who is Prince Regent?

- **Prince George** - Hugh Laurie plays the idiotic Prince George, who relies heavily on his cunning butler, Blackadder.

8. What profession does Edmund Blackadder take on in "Blackadder the Third"?

- **A butler** - Blackadder serves as the butler to the Prince Regent, manipulating him and navigating the Georgian era's court intrigues.

9. Who played the role of Queen Elizabeth I in "Blackadder II"?

- **Miranda Richardson** - Miranda Richardson's portrayal of Queen Elizabeth I is one of the highlights of the series, mixing regal authority with childish whims.

10. What is the main plot of the final episode of "Blackadder Goes Forth"?

- **An escape attempt from the trenches** - "Goodbyeee" depicts the characters' poignant and ultimately tragic attempt to escape the trenches, ending with a memorable and moving sequence.

11. What is the name of Blackadder's foolish friend in "Blackadder II"?

- **Percy** - Lord Percy, played by Tim McInnerny, is Blackadder's naive and often foolish friend.

12. Who wrote "The Black Adder" series alongside Rowan Atkinson?

- **B. Richard Curtis** - Richard Curtis co-wrote the series, bringing his sharp comedic sensibility to the scripts.

13. In "Blackadder's Christmas Carol," what role does Edmund play?

- **B. A mean man who becomes generous** - This special episode is a reversal of Charles Dickens' classic tale, showing a kind Blackadder turned mean after a visit from the Spirit of Christmas.

14. What is the name of the episode where Blackadder tries to become Archbishop of Canterbury?

- **C. "The Archbishop"** - This episode is filled with Blackadder's schemes to ascend to a high ecclesiastical office.

15. In "Blackadder II," what is the title of the episode where Blackadder must marry Princess Leia of Hungary?

- **"Bells"** - "Bells" is notable for its humorous take on mistaken identity and gender roles, with Blackadder falling for his disguised servant, Bob.

16. Who played the role of Captain Darling in "Blackadder Goes Forth"?

- **B. Tim McInnerny** - Tim McInnerny's Captain Darling is a sycophantic officer who serves as a foil to Blackadder.

17. What is the main theme of the episode "Beer" in "Blackadder II"?

- **B. Hosting a drinking contest** - Blackadder hosts a drinking contest while trying to impress his puritanical relatives, leading to hilarious results.

18. What historical period does "Blackadder the Third" take place in?

- **B. The Georgian era** - The series is set during the Regency period, focusing on the life of the Prince Regent and his butler, Blackadder.

19. What is the ultimate fate of the characters in "Blackadder Goes Forth"?

- **B. They die in battle** - The series ends with a poignant scene where the characters go "over the top" in a final, futile assault, underscoring the tragedy of war.

20. In "Blackadder II," what is Blackadder's relationship with Lord Melchett?

- B. They are rivals - Blackadder and Lord Melchett, played by Stephen Fry, often clash, with Melchett serving as one of Blackadder's many adversaries.

The Royle Family

The Royle Family: A Snapshot of British Working-Class Life

"The Royle Family" is a British television sitcom that aired from 1998 to 2000, with several specials aired in subsequent years. Created by Caroline Aherne, Craig Cash, and Henry Normal, the show presents a unique, often humorous, and sometimes poignant look at the lives of a working-class family in Manchester. Unlike many sitcoms, "The Royle Family" eschews a laugh track and instead relies on the strength of its dialogue and the depth of its characters to draw in viewers.

The show is set almost entirely in the Royles' living room, where the family members spend the majority of their time watching television, eating, and engaging in banter. The patriarch, Jim Royle (Ricky Tomlinson), is a grumpy, outspoken layabout, while his wife, Barbara (Sue Johnston), is the more sensible and nurturing figure. Their daughter, Denise (Caroline Aherne), and her husband, Dave (Craig Cash), often join in on the conversations, along with their son, Antony (Ralf Little). The show captures the essence of working-class life with its focus on everyday interactions and relatable situations.

1. **Jim Royle:** "My arse!"
   - Jim's iconic catchphrase, often used to express his disbelief or disdain.
2. **Jim Royle:** "If I had a dog with a face like yours, I'd shave its arse and teach it to walk backwards."
   - Jim's unique brand of insult, showcasing his sharp, if not crude, sense of humor.

3. **Barbara Royle:** "Antony, put that light out! What do you think this is, Blackpool illuminations?"
   - Barbara's constant worry about household expenses, reflecting the family's financial concerns.
4. **Denise Royle:** "I'm absolutely bloody starving! I've had nothing since I had that Shepherd's pie, and then a bag of chips, and then a Twix."
   - Denise's exaggeration about being hungry, highlighting her love for food and dramatic flair.
5. **Jim Royle:** "What time is it, Barbara?"
   - A frequent line used by Jim, often indicating he's waiting for something significant, like his tea or the start of a TV show.
6. **Jim Royle:** "You know what thought did? Followed a muck cart and thought it was a wedding."
   - One of Jim's many quirky sayings, showcasing his old-fashioned wisdom and humor.
7. **Dave Best:** "I'm not lazy. I'm just very relaxed."
   - Dave's laid-back attitude is perfectly encapsulated in this line, summing up his easygoing nature.
8. **Barbara Royle:** "I don't know why you watch that rubbish, Jim. You only complain about it."
   - Barbara's bemusement at Jim's habit of watching and critiquing TV shows.
9. **Denise Royle:** "Mam, what's for tea?"
   - A line frequently delivered by Denise, emphasizing her reliance on Barbara for domestic duties.
10. **Jim Royle:** "A day off? You? You have more days off than the bloody Queen's corgis."

- o Jim's sarcastic commentary on Antony's work ethic, or lack thereof.
11. **Jim Royle:** "It's only money, Barbara, you can't take it with you."
    - o Jim's nonchalant attitude towards spending, often clashing with Barbara's more frugal mindset.
12. **Barbara Royle:** "I'm just going to stick the kettle on."
    - o Barbara's go-to solution for any situation, reflecting the British love for tea.
13. **Jim Royle:** "Denise, love, would you go and get us a beer from the fridge?"
    - o Jim's frequent requests for drinks, illustrating his dependence on his family members.
14. **Norma Speakman (Nana):** "What time is it? I'll have to be getting off soon."
    - o Nana's constant concern about the time, often leading to her staying longer than planned.
15. **Antony Royle:** "I've got a job, Dad."
    - o Antony's rare but proud declarations of employment, often met with Jim's skepticism.
16. **Jim Royle:** "Freezer? We haven't got room for a bloody freezer. We'll have to put it in the bath."
    - o Jim's humorous take on the lack of space in their small home.
17. **Barbara Royle:** "Ooh, I love a bit of Gary Barlow."
    - o Barbara's celebrity crushes, particularly on the Take That singer, are a running joke.
18. **Jim Royle:** "What do you want for your tea, Barbara? We're not bleeding royalty, you know."
    - o Jim's frequent gripes about meal times and expectations.
19. **Denise Royle:** "I'll do it tomorrow."

- Denise's habitual procrastination, often to Barbara's frustration.
20. **Jim Royle:** "Marriage? It's just legalized slavery."
    - Jim's cynical view on marriage, humorously reflecting his long-standing relationship with Barbara.

"The Royle Family" stands out for its authentic depiction of working-class life and its sharp, witty dialogue. The show's ability to find humor in the mundane and its relatable characters have made it a beloved classic in British television. Through its clever writing and memorable quotes, "The Royle Family" continues to resonate with audiences, offering a humorous yet poignant look at family dynamics and everyday struggles.

Pinwright's Progress

The First Sitcom on UK TV: "Pinwright's Progress"

"Pinwright's Progress," which aired from 1946 to 1947, holds the distinction of being the first sitcom to grace British television screens. Created by Rodney Hobson and produced by the BBC, this groundbreaking show starred James Hayter as J. Pinwright, the bumbling owner of a small shop. The sitcom followed Pinwright's misadventures and his attempts to keep his business afloat despite a series of comical setbacks. The show's success set the stage for the evolution of the sitcom genre in the UK.

"Pinwright's Progress" was a trailblazer in the burgeoning television industry. Broadcasting just after World War II, it represented a shift from radio to the new medium of television. The show's format, featuring recurring characters and episodic storylines, established a template for future sitcoms. Its production, during a time when television technology was still in its infancy, required innovative techniques and a pioneering spirit from its creators and cast. The series ran for ten episodes, making it a brief but significant milestone in television history.

Before television became the dominant medium, radio comedy was the primary source of entertainment for British audiences. Shows like "ITMA" (It's That Man Again) and "Hancock's Half Hour" were immensely popular, laying the groundwork for television sitcoms. These radio comedies featured strong character-driven humor and episodic storylines, which easily transitioned to the visual medium of television. Many early TV sitcom writers and performers, including those involved in "Pinwright's Progress," came from a radio background, bringing their expertise and comedic timing to the screen.

The early days of television were fraught with challenges. Broadcasting was limited to a few hours each day, and live performances were the norm due to the lack of reliable recording technology. This meant that actors had to deliver flawless performances in real-time, often with minimal rehearsal time. The physical limitations of early TV sets, such as small screens and poor image quality, also influenced how shows were produced. Despite these hurdles, sitcoms like "Pinwright's Progress" managed to captivate audiences and demonstrate the potential of television as a medium for comedy.

Following "Pinwright's Progress," the British sitcom genre continued to evolve and flourish. The 1950s and 1960s saw the emergence of iconic shows such as "Hancock's Half Hour," which transitioned from radio to television, and "Steptoe and Son," which brought gritty realism to the sitcom format. These shows began to explore more sophisticated themes and character dynamics, reflecting the changing social landscape of post-war Britain. The success of these early sitcoms paved the way for the rich diversity of British comedy that would follow, from the surreal humor of "Monty Python's Flying Circus" to the everyday relatability of "The Royle Family."

The legacy of early British sitcoms is evident in modern television comedy. The structure, character development, and humor established by shows like "Pinwright's Progress" continue to influence contemporary sitcoms. The genre has expanded to include a wide range of styles, from the mockumentary format of "The Office" to the dark humor of "Black Mirror." The ability of sitcoms to reflect societal changes and provide commentary on contemporary issues remains a testament to the enduring appeal of the format. Today, British sitcoms are celebrated worldwide, showcasing the lasting impact of those early pioneers in television comedy.

Open All Hours

"Open All Hours" is a British television sitcom created and written by Roy Clarke, which aired from 1973 to 1985. Set in a small corner shop in Balby, South Yorkshire, the show centers around the life and antics of the miserly shopkeeper Arkwright, brilliantly portrayed by Ronnie Barker, and his long-suffering but good-natured nephew and assistant, Granville, played by David Jason. The series is known for its witty dialogue, charming character interactions, and quintessentially British humor.

The primary setting of "Open All Hours" is Arkwright's grocery shop, which serves as the perfect backdrop for the series' humor and character-driven storylines. The shop's cluttered interior, complete with old-fashioned cash register and archaic products, adds to the nostalgic and endearing atmosphere of the show. The daily operations of the shop and interactions with the local customers provide endless comedic material, reflecting the quaint charm of small-town life.

At the heart of "Open All Hours" is the dynamic between Arkwright and Granville. Arkwright is a penny-pinching, stammering shopkeeper whose primary goal is to maximize profits while minimizing expenses. His methods are often dubious and occasionally unscrupulous, but his character remains lovable due to Barker's masterful performance. Granville, on the other hand, dreams of a more exciting life away from the shop but remains loyal to his uncle. Their relationship is a blend of affection and exasperation, providing a rich source of comedy.

The shop's regular customers are an integral part of the show's humor. Characters like Nurse Gladys Emmanuel, Arkwright's love interest, bring additional layers of comedic interaction. Nurse Gladys, played by Lynda Baron, often finds herself the target of Arkwright's clumsy romantic advances, leading to numerous humorous situations. Other recurring characters, such as Mavis, Mrs. Featherstone, and various eccentric locals, add to the lively and often absurd environment of the shop.

"Open All Hours" enjoyed immense popularity during its original run and has remained a beloved classic in British television. Its enduring appeal led to a successful revival series, "Still Open All Hours," which began in 2013. The revival sees David Jason reprising his role as Granville, now running the shop himself, while retaining the charm and humor of the original series. The show's ability to resonate with audiences across generations is a testament to its timeless writing and memorable characters.

The humor in "Open All Hours" is characterized by clever wordplay, physical comedy, and the relatable absurdities of everyday life. The show's dialogue often features Arkwright's malapropisms, stammering, and sly humor, while Granville's exasperation and aspirations provide a comedic counterbalance. The simplicity of the setting and the universal nature of the characters' experiences make "Open All Hours" a comedy that continues to entertain viewers.

1. **Arkwright:** "Granville, fetch your cloth!"
    - This catchphrase became one of the most iconic lines from the show, symbolizing Arkwright's constant state of readiness to clean up any messes—literal or figurative. The phrase was often used as a prelude to a comedic situation involving a customer or mishap.
2. **Arkwright:** "It's been a very slow day. We've only had three customers and two of them were lost."
    - Reflecting the slow pace of business in the shop.
3. **Granville:** "If you don't stop treating me like a slave, I'm going to run away and join a supermarket!"
    - Granville's humorous threats to escape his mundane life.
4. **Arkwright:** "People don't like change, Granville. That's why they keep coming back to us—they know we're always the same."
    - Arkwright's ironic take on customer loyalty.

5. **Arkwright:** "She likes me for my money, Granville. The only trouble is, she knows I've got it."
   - o Arkwright's lament about Nurse Gladys' affection.
6. **Arkwright:** "Never mind the health of the nation, feel the width of their wallets."
   - o Arkwright's humorous prioritization of profits over health.
7. **Granville:** "I'm not just a shop assistant, I'm a part-time undertaker—burying Arkwright's mistakes."
   - o This line reflects Granville's sharp wit and his often overlooked intelligence. Despite being stuck in a dead-end job, Granville's cleverness shines through in his interactions with Arkwright and the customers.
8. **Arkwright:** "I'm not tight with money, Granville. I'm just very attached to it."
   - o Arkwright's defense of his frugality.
9. **Granville:** "The only thing that keeps me going is the thought of Nurse Gladys' smile... and her uniform."
   - o Granville's humorous crush on Nurse Gladys.
10. **Arkwright:** "It's a cash and carry world, Granville. You pay cash, and I carry on."
    - o The series was filmed in a real shop in Balby, Doncaster. The location added authenticity to the show, and the shop has since become a tourist attraction for fans.
11. **Arkwright:** "Granville, if you want to succeed in business, you've got to have an eye for a bargain and a hand for the till."
    - o Arkwright's advice on business success.
12. **Granville:** "I've got ambitions, you know. I don't want to be stuck here forever, smelling of pickles."
    - o David Jason's portrayal of Granville showcased his versatility as an actor. His character's dreams of

escaping the shop added depth and relatability to the series.
13. **Arkwright:** "A sale a day keeps the creditors away."
    - Arkwright's humorous business mantra.
14. **Granville:** "One of these days, I'll run this place like a proper shop—one that opens and closes at regular hours!"
    - Granville's dream of a more organized business.
15. **Arkwright:** "If you've got time to lean, you've got time to clean."
    - Arkwright's take on productivity.
16. **Granville:** "I'm just waiting for the day they invent a self-cleaning floor."
    - The show often highlighted the mundane and tedious tasks of running a small shop, which many viewers found relatable and amusing.
17. **Arkwright:** "It's not the money, Granville. It's the principle… and the money."
    - Arkwright's blend of humor and honesty about his motivations.
18. **Granville:** "I think I've spent more time dusting these shelves than living my life."
    - Granville's existential musings added a layer of depth to his character, contrasting with the show's otherwise lighthearted tone.
19. **Arkwright:** "Nurse Gladys, you're the cure for my ailments, but not for my wallet."
    - Arkwright's clumsy romantic line.
20. **Granville:** "The only way I'll get rich in this job is if I find a penny and save it for a thousand years."
    - Granville's humorous outlook on his financial prospects.

The Royle Family Quiz

Questions

1. What is the name of the head of the Royle family?

    A. Jim
    B. Bob
    C. Frank

2. Who plays Barbara Royle in the series?

    A. Sue Johnston
    B. Liz Smith
    C. Caroline Aherne

3. What is Jim Royle's famous catchphrase?

    A. "My arse!"
    B. "You plonker!"
    C. "Lovely jubbly!"

4. What is the name of Jim and Barbara's daughter?

    1. Denise
    2. Debbie
    3. Donna

5. Who is Denise married to?

    A. Dave
    B. Mick
    C. Anthony

6. What does Jim often complain about paying for?

    A. The telephone bill
    B. The TV license

C. The heating

7. What is the name of Denise and Dave's son?

A. Darren
B. David Jr.
C. Little David

8. What is Twiggy's real name?

A. Tom
B. Trevor
C. Tim

9. What job does Dave have?

A. Window cleaner
B. Taxi driver
C. Builder

10. What snack is Jim often seen eating?

A. Crisps
B. Biscuits
C. Pork scratchings

11. What game does the family often play at Christmas?

A. Monopoly
B. Trivial Pursuit
C. Scrabble

12. Who played Nana, Barbara's mother?

A. Liz Smith
B. June Whitfield
C. Thora Hird

13. What is Antony Royle's nickname given by Jim?

A. Lanky
B. Shifty
C. Lurker

14. What does Barbara often do while watching TV?

   A. Knit
   B. Iron
   C. Sew

15. What's the name of Antony's first girlfriend seen in the series?

   A. Emma
   B. Sarah
   C. Lucy

16. Which actress co-created the show along with Craig Cash?

   A. Caroline Aherne
   B. Sue Johnston
   C. Sheridan Smith

17. Where is the Royle family's home set?

   A. Manchester
   B. Liverpool
   C. Birmingham

18. What often happens to the TV in the Royle household?

   A. It breaks
   B. It gets stuck on one channel
   C. The aerial needs adjusting

19. What is Jim's favorite TV show?

   A. Coronation Street
   B. Emmerdale
   C. EastEnders

20. What do the Royles typically have for Sunday dinner?

   A. Roast beef
   B. Fish and chips
   C. Spaghetti Bolognese

The Royle Family Quiz - Answers with Additional Information

1. A. Jim
- Jim Royle, played by Ricky Tomlinson, is the grumpy patriarch known for his laziness and sarcastic humor.

2. A. Sue Johnston
- Sue Johnston portrays Barbara Royle, the loving and long-suffering wife of Jim.

3. A. "My arse!"
- This catchphrase is Jim's go-to response to almost everything, reflecting his general disdain and disbelief.

4. A. Denise
- Denise Royle, played by Caroline Aherne, is known for her lack of interest in domestic chores and her constant complaints.

5. A. Dave
- Denise is married to Dave Best, played by Craig Cash, who is known for his simple and easy-going nature.

6. B. The TV license
- Jim frequently grumbles about the cost of the TV license, despite spending most of his time watching TV.

7. C. Little David
- Denise and Dave name their son David Jr., often referred to as "Little David."

8. B. Trevor
- Twiggy, a friend of the family, is actually named Trevor. He's known for his somewhat dodgy dealings.

9. B. Taxi driver
- Dave works as a taxi driver, often sharing humorous anecdotes about his passengers.

10. B. Biscuits
- Jim is often seen munching on biscuits while watching TV.

11. B. Trivial Pursuit
- The family's Christmas games of Trivial Pursuit often lead to hilarious and heated exchanges.

12. A. Liz Smith
- Liz Smith played Nana, Barbara's sweet but sometimes sharp-tongued mother.

13. C. Lurker
- Jim refers to Antony as "Lurker," mocking his tendency to hover around doing nothing.

14. B. Iron
- Barbara is frequently seen ironing while watching TV, a nod to her role as the family's hardworking matriarch.

15. A. Emma
- Emma is Antony's first girlfriend introduced in the series, leading to some humorous and awkward moments.

16. A. Caroline Aherne
- Caroline Aherne co-created the show with Craig Cash, in addition to playing Denise.

17. A. Manchester
- The Royle family's home is set in Manchester, adding to the show's authentic Northern England feel.

18. C. The aerial needs adjusting

- The TV aerial often needs adjusting, leading to humorous scenes with the family struggling to get a clear picture.

19. A. Coronation Street

- Jim's favorite soap opera is "Coronation Street," fitting with the show's setting in the North of England.

20. A. Roast beef

- The Royle family typically has a traditional roast beef dinner on Sundays, reflecting their working-class roots.

Only Fools and Horses Quiz

Questions

1. **What is the name of the tower block where the Trotters live?**

    A. Nelson Mandela House
    B. Churchill House
    C. Gandhi House

2. **What is Del Boy's full name?**

    A. Derek Jason Trotter
    B. Derek David Trotter
    C. Derek Edward Trotter

3. **What is Rodney's middle name?**

    A. Charlton
    B. Charles
    C. Christopher

4. **What does Del Boy famously say when he falls through the bar?**

    A. "Lovely jubbly!"
    B. "Play it cool, Trig."
    C. "Cushty!"

5. **Who is Del Boy's best friend?**

    A. Boycie
    B. Denzil
    C. Trigger

6. **What is the name of Rodney's first wife?**

    A. Cassandra
    B. Raquel

C. Janice

7. What kind of vehicle do the Trotters famously drive?

    A. A yellow Ford Escort
    B. A yellow Reliant Regal
    C. A yellow Mini Cooper

8. What is Uncle Albert's catchphrase?

    A. "During the war..."
    B. "You plonker!"
    C. "Lovely jubbly!"

9. What is the name of Boycie's wife?

    A. Marlene
    B. Pauline
    C. Darlene

10. What is the name of Del and Raquel's son?

    A. David
    B. Damian
    C. Derek

11. In what year did "Only Fools and Horses" first air?

    A. 1981
    B. 1983
    C. 1985

12. What is the title of the episode where Del and Rodney dress as Batman and Robin?

    A. "Heroes and Villains"
    B. "The Longest Night"
    C. "Time on Our Hands"

13. What is the name of the local pub the Trotters frequent?

    A. The Nag's Head
    B. The Queen Vic
    C. The Red Lion

14. What did Del Boy and Rodney find that made them millionaires?

    A. A diamond ring

    B. An antique watch

    C. A rare painting

15. What was the name of Rodney's band?

    A. A Bunch of Wallies

    B. A Bunch of Plonkers

    C. A Bunch of Jollies

16. What is Grandad's first name?

    A. Edward

    B. Albert

    C. Ted

17. In which episode does Del Boy win a holiday to Margate?

    A. "Jolly Boys' Outing"

    B. "No Greater Love"

    C. "Chain Gang"

18. Who is the original actor who played Grandad?

    A. Leonard Pierce

    B. Lennard Pearce

    C. Kenneth MacDonald

19. What is Del Boy's favorite French phrase?

    A. "Au revoir"

    B. "Bonnet de douche"

    C. "Mange tout"

20. What is the name of Rodney and Cassandra's daughter?

    A. Joan

    B. Emma

    C. Emily

Answers

1. A. Nelson Mandela House

- The Trotters live in the fictional Nelson Mandela House in Peckham, London.

2. C. Derek Edward Trotter

- Del Boy's full name is Derek Edward Trotter, often shortened to Del.

3. A. Charlton

- Rodney's full name is Rodney Charlton Trotter, named after the football team Charlton Athletic.

4. B. "Play it cool, Trig."

- Del Boy famously says "Play it cool, Trig" just before falling through the bar in one of the series' most iconic moments.

5. C. Trigger

- Trigger, played by Roger Lloyd-Pack, is Del Boy's dim-witted but loyal best friend.

6. A. Cassandra

- Rodney marries Cassandra Parry, played by Gwyneth Strong.

7. B. A yellow Reliant Regal

- The Trotters drive a yellow Reliant Regal Supervan III, which becomes one of the show's symbols.

8. A. "During the war..."

- Uncle Albert, played by Buster Merryfield, often starts his stories with "During the war..."

9. A. Marlene

- Marlene, played by Sue Holderness, is Boycie's wife and known for her glamorous appearance.

10. B. Damian

- Del Boy and Raquel name their son Damian Derek Trotter.

11. A. 1981

- "Only Fools and Horses" first aired on September 8, 1981.

12. A. "Heroes and Villains"

- The episode where Del and Rodney dress as Batman and Robin is "Heroes and Villains."

13. A. The Nag's Head

- The Trotters frequent The Nag's Head, their local pub.

14. B. An antique watch

- The Trotters find a Harrison marine timekeeper, which makes them millionaires in the episode "Time on Our Hands."

15. A. A Bunch of Wallies

- Rodney's band is called A Bunch of Wallies.

16. A. Edward

- Grandad's first name is Edward, though he's mostly known just as Grandad.

17. A. "Jolly Boys' Outing"

- In the episode "Jolly Boys' Outing," Del wins a holiday to Margate.

18. B. Lennard Pearce

- The original actor who played Grandad is Lennard Pearce.

19. C. "Mange tout"

- Del Boy frequently uses the phrase "Mange tout," believing it to mean "no problem."

20. B. Joan

- Rodney and Cassandra's daughter is named Joan, after Rodney's late mother.

Peep Show: A Revolutionary British Sitcom

"Peep Show," a British sitcom that aired from 2003 to 2015, is celebrated for its innovative style and unique premise. Created by Jesse Armstrong and Sam Bain, the show revolves around the lives of two dysfunctional friends, Mark Corrigan and Jeremy "Jez" Usbourne, who share a flat in Croydon. Mark, portrayed by David Mitchell, is a socially awkward loan manager with a pessimistic outlook on life. Jez, played by Robert Webb, is a laid-back, jobless musician with dreams of fame. The dynamic between the highly strung, conservative Mark and the hedonistic, free-spirited Jez drives much of the show's humor and conflict.

What sets "Peep Show" apart from other sitcoms is its use of first-person perspective and internal monologues. The audience sees the world through the eyes of Mark and Jez, with each scene shot from their point of view. This approach allows viewers to hear the characters' unfiltered thoughts, adding a layer of depth and intimacy to the comedy. The internal monologues reveal the characters' insecurities, desires, and often contradictory thoughts, providing a brutally honest look at their personalities.

The writing in "Peep Show" is sharp, dark, and often painfully relatable. The show excels at depicting the minutiae of everyday life, from workplace politics to romantic entanglements, all while maintaining a biting satirical edge. The dialogue is laced with wit and irony, with Mark and Jez often finding themselves in hilariously awkward and morally questionable situations. The show's humor is both cerebral and crude, making it appealing to a wide audience.

The supporting cast of "Peep Show" is equally memorable, with characters like the eccentric Super Hans, the long-suffering Sophie, and the domineering Johnson adding to the comedic landscape. Each character is well-developed and brings their own brand of humor to the show. The interactions between the main and supporting characters are rife with tension, misunderstandings, and hilarious consequences, further enriching the series.

"Peep Show" also explores deeper themes such as loneliness, failure, and the search for meaning in modern life. Despite their flaws and often selfish behavior, Mark and Jez's friendship provides a sense of stability and companionship. The show's ability to balance comedy with poignant moments of vulnerability and existential angst is one of its greatest strengths. This balance ensures that while viewers are laughing at the absurdity of the characters' lives, they are also empathizing with their struggles.

Overall, "Peep Show" is a groundbreaking sitcom that combines innovative filming techniques, sharp writing, and memorable characters. Its exploration of modern life's absurdities, coupled with its distinctive style, has earned it a dedicated fan base and critical acclaim. The show's influence can be seen in many subsequent comedies that attempt to blend dark humor with relatable, everyday scenarios.

1. Mark: "I have a plan. It's a three-point plan. A. I steal some booze. B. I get you drunk. C. I have sex with you. D. I steal some more booze."

- Mark's awkward and creepy attempt to seduce Sophie.

2. Jeremy: "I'm just a normal functioning member of the human race and there's no way anyone can prove otherwise."

- Jez's self-delusion at its finest.

3. Super Hans: "People like Coldplay and voted for the Nazis. You can't trust people."

- Super Hans' unique take on popular culture and democracy.

4. **Mark:** "The bad thing about crossing the line is when you've crossed it, you don't even know you've done it."

- Mark's reflection on his moral failings.

5. **Jeremy:** "Oh my God, a snakebite! I'm gonna die! This is outrageous! How many more of us have to get bitten before you get a gardener?"

- Jez's ridiculous overreaction to a bee sting.

6. **Mark:** "Sophie's mom is a MILF. No, a GMILF. God, I am one sick f*."

- Mark's inappropriate thoughts about Sophie's mom.

7. **Jeremy:** "It's not really a pyramid scheme. It's more of a... triangle."

- Jez trying to justify a dodgy business venture.

8. **Mark:** "She's my dream woman. Big teeth, skinny ankles, not mental. God, I hope she doesn't think I'm mental."

- Mark's odd criteria for his perfect partner.

9. **Jeremy:** "It's not about the money. It's about the music. And the money."

- Jez's priorities in a nutshell.

11. **Jeremy:** "There's no way I'm getting a job. Jobs are for mugs."

- Jez's attitude towards employment.

12. **Mark:** "I suppose doing things you hate is just the price you pay to avoid loneliness."

- Mark's grim outlook on life.

13. **Super Hans:** "The secret ingredient is crime."

- Super Hans on what makes a business successful.

14. Jeremy: "The thing about destiny is, it never ever works out, not really."

- Jez on the futility of relying on destiny.

15. Mark: "I'm doing the work of two men. Unfortunately, they're Laurel and Hardy."

- Mark's frustration with his workload.

16. Jeremy: "I can't go to prison, Mark. They'll rape the pants off me!"

- Jez's exaggerated fear of prison.

17. Mark: "I'm permanently scared, I've learnt to accept it."

- Mark's admission of his constant anxiety.

18. Super Hans: "A gig's a gig. It's not about the music, it's about the rhythm. It's tribal."

- Super Hans' unconventional view on performing.

19. Jeremy: "It's fine to lie in small doses. It's like a pie; you don't have a whole pie."

- Jez justifying his dishonest behavior.

20. Mark: "God, I'm the boring one. I'm the office brown-noser. I'm a bland, nothing person."

- Mark's moment of self-realization and despair.

Gavin & Stacey: The Charm of Everyday Life

"Gavin & Stacey," a British sitcom that aired from 2007 to 2010, became a cultural phenomenon due to its relatable characters, heartfelt storytelling, and clever blend of humor and drama. Created by James Corden and Ruth Jones, the show focuses on the romance between Gavin, from Essex, and Stacey, from Wales, and the ensuing relationships between their friends and families. Here are some reasons why "Gavin & Stacey" resonated with audiences and a few memorable moments from the series.

One of the primary reasons "Gavin & Stacey" became so popular is the authenticity of its characters and relationships. The show brilliantly portrays the complexities of family dynamics and friendships. Gavin (Mathew Horne) and Stacey (Joanna Page) are incredibly relatable as a young couple navigating the challenges of a long-distance relationship. Their friends, Smithy (James Corden) and Nessa (Ruth Jones), as well as their families, add depth and humor to the narrative. Each character is well-developed and feels like someone you might know in real life.

The show balances humor with genuine emotion, making it more than just a sitcom. It explores themes of love, friendship, family, and the ups and downs of everyday life. The humor is often derived from the characters' interactions and the situations they find themselves in, which are both funny and touching. This mix of comedy and heartfelt moments ensures that the show resonates with a wide audience.

Memorable Moments

1. **Smithy's Indian Takeaway Order**
   - One of the most iconic scenes is Smithy's elaborate takeaway order, showcasing his indecisive nature and love for food. His detailed list of items is both hilarious and relatable to anyone who has struggled with decision-making.

2. **Nessa's Unexpected Pregnancy**
   - The revelation of Nessa's pregnancy is a pivotal moment in the series. Her blunt announcement to Smithy and the subsequent reactions from both families provide a mix of shock, humor, and heartfelt responses.

3. **The Barn Dance**
   - The barn dance in Barry Island is a memorable and joyous episode that highlights the cultural differences between Gavin and Stacey's families. The dance-off between Smithy and Nessa is particularly entertaining.

4. **Pam's Vegan Christmas**
   - Pam (Alison Steadman) attempting to cook a vegan Christmas dinner for Mick (Larry Lamb) leads to a series of comedic mishaps, perfectly illustrating her loving but often misguided efforts to please her family.

5. Gavin and Stacey's Wedding

- The wedding episode is a beautifully crafted mix of humor and emotion. The various mishaps and touching moments during the ceremony and reception capture the essence of the show's charm.

The supporting cast of "Gavin & Stacey" is crucial to its success. Characters like Bryn (Rob Brydon), with his quirky yet lovable personality, and Doris (Margaret John), with her cheeky one-liners, add layers of humor and warmth to the show. Each supporting character is given enough screen time and development to feel integral to the storyline, enriching the main narrative with their unique traits.

The show's setting in both Essex and Barry Island allows it to explore and celebrate the cultural differences between the English and Welsh characters. This dual setting provides a backdrop for comedic moments and misunderstandings while also highlighting the universality of family and friendship.

Despite ending in 2010, "Gavin & Stacey" has retained its popularity due to its timeless themes and relatable humor. The show's revival for a Christmas special in 2019 was met with widespread excitement, proving its lasting impact. The special episode, filled with nostalgia and new laughs, reminded fans why they fell in love with the show in the first place.

Outnumbered: A Unique Take on Family Life

"Outnumbered," which aired from 2007 to 2016, stands out in the British sitcom landscape for its realistic portrayal of family life and its innovative use of semi-improvised dialogue. Created by Andy Hamilton and Guy Jenkin, the show centers on the Brockman family and captures the chaotic, humorous, and often touching moments of everyday life with young children. Here's an exploration of why "Outnumbered" became so popular, how it differentiates itself from other sitcoms, and some interesting facts about the show.

"Outnumbered" resonated with audiences primarily because of its authentic depiction of family life. The Brockman family, consisting of parents Pete (Hugh Dennis) and Sue (Claire Skinner), and their three children, Jake (Tyger Drew-Honey), Ben (Daniel Roche), and Karen (Ramona Marquez), navigate the trials and tribulations of parenting with humor and honesty. The show's ability to capture the small, everyday moments and the larger, more chaotic episodes of family life made it relatable to viewers of all ages.

One of the most distinctive features of "Outnumbered" is its use of semi-improvised dialogue. The child actors were given outlines and prompts rather than strict scripts, allowing for spontaneous and natural interactions. This technique resulted in genuine, often hilarious performances that perfectly captured the unpredictability of children. The adults, especially Dennis and Skinner, had to react in real-time to the children's improvisations, adding to the authenticity of the show.

"Outnumbered" strikes a perfect balance between humor and heartfelt moments. The comedic aspects often arise from the children's innocent yet brutally honest remarks, the parents' exasperation, and the everyday mishaps that occur in a bustling household. Alongside the humor, the show also delves into deeper issues such as parenting challenges, marital strains, and the bittersweet passage of time, providing a well-rounded portrayal of family life.

1. Karen's Inquisitiveness

- Karen's relentless questioning and unique perspective on the world lead to some of the show's funniest and most thought-provoking moments. Her curiosity often puts her parents in awkward situations, showcasing the challenges of answering a child's unfiltered questions.

2. Ben's Wild Imagination

- Ben's boundless energy and vivid imagination result in numerous comedic scenarios. Whether he's convinced he's a superhero or coming up with elaborate stories, his antics are a constant source of humor.

3. Jake's Teenage Angst

- As the eldest child, Jake's experiences with teenage angst, school pressures, and early romantic interests provide a relatable and often humorous depiction of adolescence.

4. The Holiday Episodes

- Episodes featuring the family's attempts at holiday outings, such as camping trips or visits to relatives, highlight the often chaotic nature of family vacations, filled with mishaps and misunderstandings.

5. Parent-Teacher Meetings

- The Brockmans' interactions with teachers and school authorities offer a comedic look at the educational system and the challenges parents face in navigating it.

"Outnumbered" differentiates itself from other sitcoms through its unique format and approach to storytelling. The semi-improvised dialogue gives the show a fresh, unscripted feel that stands in contrast to the tightly scripted nature of many traditional sitcoms. Additionally, its focus on the genuine, often mundane aspects of family life, rather than exaggerated scenarios, sets it apart. The show's ability to blend humor with heartfelt, realistic portrayals of parenting challenges has earned it critical acclaim and a dedicated fanbase.

The Black Adder: A Unique Comedy Journey

"The Black Adder," a British sitcom that aired from 1983 to 1989, is renowned for its sharp wit, historical settings, and memorable characters. Created by Richard Curtis and Rowan Atkinson, the series follows the exploits of various incarnations of Edmund Blackadder across different historical periods. Each series presents a different era, starting with the medieval period in "The Black Adder," moving to the Elizabethan era in "Blackadder II," the Regency period in "Blackadder the Third," and finally, the First World War in "Blackadder Goes Forth." The show is celebrated for its clever satire, dark humor, and the evolving character of Blackadder, who becomes progressively more cunning and cynical with each series.

One of the defining features of "The Black Adder" is its combination of historical settings with modern comedic sensibilities. The show blends historical references and events with contemporary humor, creating a unique and engaging experience for the audience. Rowan Atkinson's portrayal of Edmund Blackadder is central to the series' success, with each incarnation of Blackadder being a scheming, sarcastic anti-hero surrounded by a cast of equally memorable characters. Baldrick, Blackadder's dim-witted servant, played by Tony Robinson, provides a perfect foil to Blackadder's intelligence and wit, contributing to some of the series' funniest moments.

The show's influence on British comedy is significant, as it introduced a new level of sophistication to sitcoms with its historical settings and intelligent humor. "The Black Adder" is not just a comedy but also a commentary on power, class, and human nature. The series' ability to blend humor with poignant moments, particularly in the final episode of "Blackadder Goes Forth," where the characters meet their tragic fate, highlights its depth and versatility. "The Black Adder" remains a classic, revered for its clever writing, superb performances, and its ability to entertain and provoke thought in equal measure.

- **Royal Approval**: Prince Charles is a fan of the series and once invited the cast to perform a sketch for his 40th birthday.
- **Pilot Episode**: There was an unaired pilot episode with significant differences, including the character of Baldrick being smarter than Blackadder.
- **Historical Inaccuracies**: The show intentionally includes historical inaccuracies for comedic effect, such as placing real historical figures in fictional scenarios.
- **Alternate Titles**: The show was almost called "The Black Vegetable" before "The Black Adder" was chosen.
- **Baldrick's Turnip**: Baldrick's obsession with turnips was inspired by an actual 18th-century belief that turnips could be used to predict the future.
- **Expensive Production**: The first series was one of the most expensive sitcoms ever made due to its elaborate sets and costumes.
- **Script Rewrites**: Richard Curtis and Ben Elton would often rewrite scripts just hours before filming to ensure the jokes were as sharp as possible.
- **Lost Manuscript**: An entire script for "Blackadder II" was lost on a train by Richard Curtis and had to be rewritten from scratch.
- **Stephen Fry's Lineage**: Stephen Fry, who plays Lord Melchett, is actually distantly related to an actual historical figure who served Queen Elizabeth I.
- **Final Episode Impact**: The final episode of "Blackadder Goes Forth" is credited with significantly raising awareness and changing perceptions about World War I in the UK.

Funniest One-Liners and Gags from "The Black Adder"

Blackadder: "Baldrick, your head is as empty as a eunuch's underpants."

Baldrick: "I have a cunning plan!"

Blackadder: "I have a plan so cunning you could put a tail on it and call it a weasel."

Blackadder: "This is a crisis. A large crisis. In fact, if you've got a moment, it's a twelve-story crisis with a magnificent entrance hall, carpeting throughout, 24-hour porterage, and an enormous sign on the roof, saying 'This Is a Large Crisis.'"

Baldrick: "Permission to shout 'bravo' at an annoyingly loud volume, sir?"

Blackadder: "I'm as happy as a Frenchman who's just invented a pair of self-removing trousers."

Blackadder: "I couldn't be more petrified if a wild rhinoceros had just come home from a hard day at the swamp, found me in his pyjamas, and was now looking at me in a funny way."

Blackadder: "The path of my life is strewn with cowpats from the devil's own satanic herd."

Baldrick: "My family's history isn't all heroic, you know. I had an uncle at the Battle of Hastings who fought on the wrong side."

Blackadder: "We're in the stickiest situation since Sticky the Stick Insect got stuck on a sticky bun."

Melchett: "If nothing else works, a total pig-headed unwillingness to look facts in the face will see us through."

Blackadder: "Baldrick, you wouldn't recognise a subtle plan if it painted itself purple and danced naked on a harpsichord, singing 'Subtle Plans Are Here Again.'"

Blackadder: "Am I jumping the gun, Baldrick, or are the words 'I have a cunning plan' marching with ill-deserved confidence in the direction of this conversation?"

Blackadder: "Baldrick, I think I've been rather too harsh on you these last seventeen years. In order to make amends, I'm going to buy you a delightful new codpiece in the shape of a turnip."

Blackadder: "In the court of Elizabeth I, if you were tall and handsome, you'd go far. If you were short and funny, you'd go further."

Baldrick: "I've been in your service since I was two-and-a-half, my lord. Well, I must've started late."

Blackadder: "A war hasn't been fought this badly since Olaf the Hairy, High Chief of all the Vikings, accidentally ordered 80,000 battle helmets with the horns on the inside."

Blackadder: "Never had anything you can't rip the roof off, throw away half, and still get a full meal out of."

Blackadder: "I trust you had a pleasant evening? Not many people get to meet their executioner a night early."

Blackadder: "To you, Baldrick, the Renaissance was just something that happened to other people, wasn't it?"

The Vicar of Dibley: A Heartwarming Comedy

"The Vicar of Dibley" is a beloved British sitcom that aired from 1994 to 2007, with special episodes extending into 2015. Created by Richard Curtis, the show stars Dawn French as Geraldine Granger, the vivacious and unconventional female vicar who takes over the parish of the small fictional village of Dibley. The series was groundbreaking for its time, addressing gender roles within the church while delivering a hearty dose of humor. Geraldine's efforts to win over the initially skeptical parish council and her interactions with the quirky villagers create the foundation for the show's humor and heart.

The strength of "The Vicar of Dibley" lies in its ensemble cast, each bringing their own unique quirks and charm to the village. Characters like the bumbling but lovable Hugo Horton (James Fleet), his domineering mother Alice (Emma Chambers), and the grumpy David Horton (Gary Waldhorn) add depth and humor to the series. The show expertly blends slapstick comedy with clever dialogue, often highlighting the contrast between Geraldine's modern views and the villagers' traditional ways. Over the years, the series evolved to include touching moments and social commentary, making it more than just a comedy but a beloved part of British television culture.

The series is renowned for its Christmas and Easter specials, which became highly anticipated events. These specials often featured celebrity cameos and tackled larger themes, while maintaining the show's trademark humor. "The Vicar of Dibley" also made a significant cultural impact by normalizing the presence of women in clergy roles at a time when the Church of England was still coming to terms with female vicars. The show's enduring popularity is a testament to its charming characters, witty writing, and the warmth it brings to audiences.

Funniest Gags and Moments from "The Vicar of Dibley"

- **The Arrival**: Geraldine's unexpected arrival and the council's shock at having a female vicar.
- **Easter Bunny**: Geraldine dressing up as the Easter Bunny and hilariously scaring the children.
- **Chocolate Addiction**: Geraldine's humorous struggles with her chocolate addiction, leading to numerous comedic situations.
- **Hugo's Proposal**: Hugo's bumbling proposal to Alice, including miscommunications and awkward moments.
- **The Wedding**: The chaotic and heartwarming wedding of Hugo and Alice, filled with mishaps and laughs.
- **Alice's Cluelessness**: Alice's various misunderstandings and innocent comments, especially her confusion over Geraldine's jokes.
- **The Songs of Praise Episode**: The villagers' hilarious attempts to appear pious for the TV cameras.
- **The Water Splash**: The running gag of Geraldine falling into a puddle that is much deeper than it appears.
- **Celebrity Cameos**: Special episodes featuring cameos from stars like Johnny Depp and Kylie Minogue.
- **David Horton's Soft Side**: Moments when the grumpy David Horton shows his softer side, especially towards his son Hugo.
- **The Christmas Lunch Incident**: Geraldine ends up eating multiple Christmas dinners after accepting too many invitations.
- **The French Lesson**: Geraldine's disastrous attempt to teach the villagers French.

- **The Nativity Play**: The hilariously chaotic Nativity play put on by the villagers.
- **Owen's Unfiltered Comments**: Owen's blunt and often inappropriate remarks that always catch Geraldine off guard.
- **Geraldine's Bridesmaid Dress**: The hideous bridesmaid dress Geraldine is forced to wear at Alice's wedding.
- **The Talking Animal**: Geraldine's reaction to the revelation of a talking animal in the village.
- **Dibley Radio**: The villagers' inept attempt to run a local radio station.
- **Geraldine's Love Life**: Geraldine's awkward and humorous attempts at dating.
- **Alice's Fancy Dress**: Alice's absurd fancy dress costumes at various village events.
- **The Final Episode**: The touching and hilarious finale, where Geraldine leads the village in a tribute to the late Alice.

Did You Know?

- **Real-Life Inspiration**: The character of Geraldine Granger was inspired by Joy Carroll, one of the first female vicars in the Church of England.
- **Guest Stars**: The show featured several celebrity guest stars, including Johnny Depp, Kylie Minogue, and Sarah Ferguson, Duchess of York.
- **Emma Chambers' Impact**: Emma Chambers, who played Alice Tinker, was awarded the British Comedy Award for Best Actress for her role.
- **Dawn French's Dedication**: Dawn French gained weight for the role, believing it would add to the character's jolly, larger-than-life personality.
- **Charity Specials**: The show produced special episodes for charity events like Comic Relief, which were immensely popular and raised significant funds.

Porridge: A Classic British Sitcom

"Porridge" is a beloved British sitcom that originally aired from 1974 to 1977. Created by the legendary writing duo Dick Clement and Ian La Frenais, the show is set in the fictional HMP Slade, a prison in Cumberland. The series stars Ronnie Barker as Norman Stanley Fletcher, an experienced and cunning inmate serving a five-year sentence for burglary. Alongside him is Richard Beckinsale as Lennie Godber, a naive and good-hearted young prisoner whom Fletcher takes under his wing.

The show cleverly balances humor with the harsh realities of prison life, making it both a comedy and a subtle commentary on the British penal system. Fletcher's wit, wisdom, and ability to manipulate the system provide much of the show's humor, while Godber's innocence and optimism offer a contrasting perspective. The supporting cast, including Fulton Mackay as the strict but fair prison officer Mr. Mackay and Brian Wilde as the more lenient Mr. Barrowclough, add depth and additional layers of comedy to the series.

"Porridge" is celebrated for its sharp writing, memorable characters, and the exceptional performance of Ronnie Barker. The show's ability to find humor in the bleakest of circumstances, along with its endearing characters, has made it a timeless classic. Its blend of situational comedy and character-driven humor continues to resonate with audiences, demonstrating the resilience and camaraderie of its characters despite the confines of prison life.

Funniest One-Liners and Moments from "Porridge"

- **Fletcher:** "I read a book once. Green it was, with a red cover."
- **Godber:** "Do you think I'll ever become institutionalized?"
  Fletcher: "What, you mean become part of the furniture? You already are, son, you already are."
- **Mr. Mackay:** "You're a born leader, Fletcher."
- **Fletcher:** "Yes, Mr. Mackay, but I was leading myself astray."
- **Fletcher:** "You can't educate pork."
- **Godber:** "I'm innocent!"
- **Fletcher:** "Of course you are. Just like everybody else in here."
- **Fletcher:** "When you've been inside as long as I have, you realize that the one thing you need to survive is patience."
  Godber: "How long have you been in then?"
- **Fletcher:** "Three days."
- **Fletcher:** "Prison is like life, with all the bad bits taken out."
- **Fletcher:** "Never make the same mistake twice. Unless it pays."
- **Fletcher:** "The only exercise I take is walking behind the coffins of friends who took exercise."
- **Fletcher:** "They say walls have ears. But sometimes they have mouths as well."
- **Mr. Mackay:** "There are two ways to do things in this prison: my way or the hard way."
- **Fletcher:** "What's the difference?"
- **Mr. Mackay:** "The hard way hurts more."
- **Fletcher:** "Always remember: the screw who searches you doesn't like doing it any more than you like being searched."
- **Godber:** "Do you ever think about the outside, Fletch?"
  Fletcher: "Only when I'm not thinking about the inside."

- **Fletcher:** "In here, hope is what keeps you going. It's the lack of it that finishes you."
- **Fletcher:** "There are only two types of people in this prison: the quick and the dead."
- **Fletcher:** "If brains were taxed, you'd get a rebate."
- **Godber:** "I suppose there's no point in getting depressed about being in here."
- **Fletcher:** "No point at all, son. If you're feeling low, just think of Mr. Mackay – he's got to stay here forever."
- **Fletcher:** "Every day's the same, see? And what makes it worse is, every night's the same as well."
- **Fletcher:** "In here, even the losers win sometimes."
- **Fletcher:** "Just remember, son, laughter is the best medicine. Unless you've got something serious, in which case you'll need proper medicine."

The Good Life: 10 Crazy and Interesting Facts

1. **Realistic Farming**: Richard Briers and Felicity Kendal, who played Tom and Barbara Good, actually learned how to handle animals and grow vegetables to make their portrayal of self-sufficient life as realistic as possible. They spent time on farms to get hands-on experience.
2. **Celebrity Fans**: The show garnered a surprising fanbase, including members of the British royal family. It is reported that Queen Elizabeth II and Prince Philip were avid viewers and even invited the cast to Buckingham Palace for a dinner.
3. **On-Set Mishaps**: During filming, Richard Briers was often injured while handling the various farm animals and equipment. One notable incident involved him getting nipped by a goat, leading to a temporary halt in filming.
4. **Paul Eddington's Allergies**: Paul Eddington, who played the Goods' posh neighbor Jerry Leadbetter, was allergic to many of the animals used in the series. Despite this, he maintained his professionalism and continued filming, often needing antihistamines to get through scenes.
5. **Felicity Kendal's Popularity**: Felicity Kendal, playing Barbara Good, became an unexpected sex symbol in the 1970s. Her character's combination of charm, practicality, and good looks won her a massive following, leading to numerous magazine covers and interviews.
6. **Real-Life Friendship**: The chemistry between the characters wasn't just for the cameras. The main cast members, particularly Richard Briers and Penelope Keith (Margo Leadbetter), became close friends off-screen. Their genuine

camaraderie contributed significantly to the show's warm and relatable feel.
7. **Eco-Friendly Influence**: The show inspired a real-life movement towards self-sufficiency and eco-friendly living in the UK. Many viewers started their own gardens, keeping chickens, and adopting sustainable practices inspired by the Goods' lifestyle.
8. **Unintended Prop Damage**: The scenes featuring Margo's garden were often filmed in real suburban gardens. During one shoot, the crew accidentally damaged a neighbor's prize-winning roses, leading to a tense situation that had to be resolved with compensation and profuse apologies.
9. **Famous Guest Stars**: "The Good Life" featured several famous guest stars, including tennis legend John McEnroe, who appeared in a dream sequence. His cameo added an extra layer of surreal humor to the show.
10. **Influence on Future Shows**: "The Good Life" set a precedent for future British sitcoms exploring alternative lifestyles. Shows like "The Good Life" paved the way for series like "Green Wing" and "The Office" by blending humor with everyday struggles and triumphs, influencing a generation of television writers and producers.

A Love Letter to British Sitcoms

As we draw the curtains on this journey through the delightful world of British sitcoms, it's clear that these shows have left an indelible mark on the fabric of television history. From the lovable misfits of "Only Fools and Horses" to the razor-sharp satire of "Yes Minister," each series has brought something uniquely British to our screens, capturing the humor, heart, and quirks of everyday life in the UK.

These sitcoms are more than just entertainment; they are cultural touchstones that have united generations in laughter. They remind us of the power of comedy to reflect our society, challenge our norms, and, most importantly, bring us together.

So, as you finish this book, we hope you've enjoyed reminiscing about your favorite shows and perhaps even discovered a few new ones to love. Now, with a cup of tea in hand and a smile on your face, why not take on *The Ultimate British Sitcom Challenge*? Scan the QR code for free trivia content, join the fun, and let's celebrate the shows that have made us laugh for decades.

And finally, thank you for being a part of this journey. If you've enjoyed this exploration of British comedy, we'd love to hear your thoughts. Please take a moment to leave a review—it's the perfect way to keep the laughter going!

Printed in Great Britain
by Amazon